WORDS of WAR and PEACE

WORDS

GREAT SPEECHES OF
WAR, CONFLICT, AND
MILITARY HISTORY

of

WAR and

PEACE

pac ps

Pacific Publishing Studio

Published in the United States by Beacon Hill, an
imprint of Pacific Publishing Studio.
www.PacPS.com

ISBN – 978-0-9824454-2-6

To order a copy of this book, visit
www.Amazon.com.

Special acknowledgement is made to the following
Editor: Lee Prescott
Cover Photography: Big Stock Photography
Transcription: Pacific Publishing Studio

Contents

Winston Churchill

Preparation for Nazi Aggresssion
May 13, 1940

I beg to move

That this House welcomes the formation of a Government representing the united and inflexible resolve of the nation to prosecute the war with Germany to a victorious conclusion.

On Friday evening last, I received His Majesty's commission to form a new Administration. It, as the evident wish and will of Parliament and the nation, that this should be conceived on the broadest possible basis and that it should include all parties, both those who supported the late Government and also the parties of the Opposition.

I have completed the most important part of this task. A War Cabinet has been formed of five Members, representing, with the Opposition Liberals, the unity of the nation. The three party Leaders have agreed to serve, either in the War Cabinet or in high executive office. The three Fighting Services have been filled. It was necessary that this should be done in one single day, on account of the extreme urgency and rigor of events.

A number of other positions, key positions, were filled yesterday, and I am submitting a further list to His

1

Majesty tonight. I hope to complete the appointment of the principal Ministers during tomorrow. The appointment of the other Ministers usually takes a little longer, but I trust that, when Parliament meets again, this part of my task will be completed, and that the administration will be complete in all respects.

I considered it in the public interest to suggest that the House should be summoned to meet today. Mr. Speaker agreed and took the necessary steps, in accordance with the powers conferred upon him by the Resolution of the House. At the end of the proceedings today, the Adjournment of the House will be proposed until Tuesday, 21st May, with, of course, provision for earlier meeting if need be. The business to be considered during that week will be notified to Members at the earliest opportunity.

I now invite the House, by the Motion which stands in my name, to record its approval of the steps taken and to declare its confidence in the new Government.

The resolution:

"That this House welcomes the formation of a government representing the united and inflexible resolve of the nation to prosecute the war with Germany to a victorious conclusion."

To form an Administration of this scale and complexity is a serious undertaking in itself, but it must be remembered that we are in the preliminary stage of one of the greatest battles in history; that we are in action at many other points in Norway and in Holland; that we have to be prepared in the Mediterranean; that the air battle is continuous and that many preparations have to be made here at home.

In this crisis, I hope I may be pardoned if I do not address the House at any length today. I hope that any of my friends and colleagues, or former colleagues, who are affected by the political reconstruction, will make allowance, all allowance, for any lack of ceremony with which it has been necessary to act. I would say to the House, as I said to those who have joined this government: "I have nothing to offer but blood, toil, tears, and sweat."

We have before us an ordeal of the most grievous kind. We have before us many, many long months of struggle and of suffering. You ask, what is our policy?

I can say: It is to wage war by sea, land, and air, with all our might and with all the strength that God can give us; to wage war against a monstrous tyranny, never surpassed in the dark, lamentable catalogue of human crime. That is our policy.

You ask, what is our aim? I can answer in one word: It is victory, victory at all costs, victory in spite of all terror, victory, however long and hard the road may be; for without victory, there is no survival. Let that be realized; no survival for the British Empire, no survival for all that the British Empire has stood for, no survival for the urge and impulse of the ages, that mankind will move forward towards its goal.

But I take up my task with buoyancy and hope. I feel sure that our cause will not be suffered to fail among men.

At this time I feel entitled to claim the aid of all, and I say: Come then, let us go forward together with our united strength.

Dwight Eisenhower

D-Day Order
June 6, 1944

You will bring about the destruction of the German war machine, the elimination of Nazi tyranny over the oppressed peoples of Europe, and security for ourselves in a free world.

Your task will not be an easy one. Your enemy is well trained, well equipped, and battle-hardened. He will fight savagely.

But this is the year 1944. Much has happened since the Nazi triumphs of 1940-41.

The United Nations have inflicted upon the Germans great defeat in open battle man to man. Our air offensive has seriously reduced their strength in the air and their capacity to wage war on the ground.

Our home fronts have given us an overwhelming superiority in weapons and munitions of war and placed at our disposal great reserves of trained fighting men.

The tide has turned.

The free men of the world are marching together to victory. I have full confidence in your courage, devotion to duty, and skill in battle.

We will accept nothing less than full victory.

Good luck, and let us all beseech the blessings of Almighty God upon this great and noble undertaking.

Douglas MacArthur

Surrender Ceremony of Japan, U.S.S. Missouri
September 2, 1945

We are gathered here, representatives of the major warring powers, to conclude a solemn agreement whereby peace may be restored. The issues, involving divergent ideals and ideologies, have been determined on the battlefields of the world and hence are not for our discussion or debate. Nor is it for us here to meet, representing as we do a majority of the people of the earth, in a spirit of distrust, malice, or hatred. But rather, it is for us, both victors and vanquished, to rise to that higher dignity which alone befits the sacred purposes we are about to serve: committing all our people unreservedly to faithful compliance with the understanding they are here formally to assume.

It is my earnest hope and indeed the hope of all mankind, that from this solemn occasion a better world shall emerge out of the blood and carnage of the past—a world dedicated to the dignity of man and the fulfillment of his most cherished wish for freedom, tolerance and justice.

John F. Kennedy

The Bay of Pigs Invasion Address
April 20, 1961

Mr. Catledge, members of the American Society of Newspaper Editors, ladies and gentlemen:

The President of a great democracy such as ours, and the editors of great newspapers such as yours owe a common obligation to the people: an obligation to present the facts, to present them with candor, and to present them in perspective. It is with that obligation in mind that I have decided in the last 24 hours to discuss briefly at this time the recent events in Cuba.

On that unhappy island, as in so many other arenas of the contest for freedom, the news has grown worse instead of better. I have emphasized before that this was a struggle of Cuban patriots against a Cuban dictator. While we could not be expected to hide our sympathies, we made it repeatedly clear that the armed forces of this country would not intervene in any way.

Any unilateral American intervention, in the absence of an external attack upon ourselves or an ally, would have been contrary to our traditions and to our international obligations. But let the record show that our restraint is not inexhaustible. Should it ever appear that the inter-American doctrine of non-interference merely conceals or excuses a policy of non-action if the nations of this Hemisphere should fail to meet their commitments against outside Communist penetration—then I want it clearly understood that this Government will not hesitate in meeting its primary obligations which are to the security of our Nation.

Should that time ever come, we do not intend to be lectured on "intervention" by those whose character was stamped for all time on the bloody streets of Budapest! Nor would we expect or accept the same outcome which this small band of gallant Cuban refugees must have known that they were chancing, determined as they were against heavy odds to pursue their courageous attempts to regain their Island's freedom.

But Cuba is not an island unto itself; and our concern is not ended by mere expressions of non-intervention or regret. This is not the first time in either ancient or recent history that a small band of freedom fighters has engaged the armor of totalitarianism.

It is not the first time that Communist tanks have rolled over gallant men and women fighting to redeem the independence of their homeland. Nor is it by any means the final episode in the eternal struggle of liberty against tyranny, anywhere on the face of the globe, including Cuba itself.

Mr. Castro has said that these were mercenaries. According to press reports, the final message to be relayed from the refugee forces on the beach came from the rebel commander when asked if he wished to be evacuated. His answer was: "I will never leave this country." That is not the reply of a mercenary. He has gone now to join, in the mountains, countless other guerrilla fighters who are equally determined that the dedication of those who gave their lives shall not be forgotten, and that Cuba must not be abandoned to the Communists. And we do not intend to abandon it either

The Cuban people have not yet spoken their final piece. And I have no doubt that they and their Revolutionary Council, led by Dr. Cardona, and members of the families of the Revolutionary Council—I am informed by the Doctor yesterday—are involved themselves in the Islands, will continue to speak up for a free and independent Cuba.

Meanwhile, we will not accept Mr. Castro's attempts to blame this nation for the hatred which his onetime supporters now regard his repression. But there are from this sobering episode useful lessons for us all to learn. Some may be still obscure and await further information. Some are clear today.

First, it is clear that the forces of communism are not to be underestimated, in Cuba or anywhere else in the world. The advantages of a police state—its use of mass terror and arrests to prevent the spread of free

10

dissent—cannot be overlooked by those who expect the fall of every fanatic tyrant. If the self-discipline of the free cannot match the iron discipline of the mailed fist—in economic, political, scientific, and all the other kinds of struggles as well as the military—then the peril to freedom will continue to rise.

Secondly, it is clear that this Nation, in concert with all the free nations of this hemisphere, must take an ever closer and more realistic look at the menace of external Communist intervention and domination in Cuba. The American people are not complacent about Iron Curtain tanks and planes less than go miles from their shore. But a nation of Cuba's size is less a threat to our survival than it is a base for subverting the survival of other free nations throughout the hemisphere. It is not primarily our interest or our security but theirs, which is now, today, in the greater peril. It is for their sake as well as our own that we must show our will.

The evidence is clear and the hour is late. We and our Latin friends will have to face the fact that we cannot postpone any longer the real issue of survival of freedom in this hemisphere itself. On that issue, unlike perhaps some others, there can be no middle ground. Together we must build a hemisphere where freedom can flourish, and where any free nation under outside attack of any kind can be assured that all of our resources stand ready to respond to any request for assistance.

11

Third and finally, it is clearer than ever that we face a relentless struggle in every corner of the globe that goes far beyond the clash of armies or even nuclear armaments. The armies are there, and in large number. The nuclear armaments are there. But they serve primarily as the shield behind which subversion, infiltration, and a host of other tactics steadily advance, picking off vulnerable areas one by one in situations which do not permit our own armed intervention.

Power is the hallmark of this offensive power and discipline and deceit. The legitimate discontent of yearning people is exploited. The legitimate trappings of self-determination are employed. But once in power, all talk of discontent is repressed; all self-determination disappears, and the promise of a revolution of hope is betrayed, as in Cuba, into a reign of terror.

Those who, on instruction, staged automatic "riots" in the streets of free nations over the efforts of a small group of young Cubans to regain their freedom should recall the long roll call of refugees who cannot now go back to Hungary, to North Korea, to North Vietnam, to East Germany, or to Poland, or to any of the other lands from which a steady stream of refugees pours forth, in eloquent testimony to the cruel oppression now holding sway in their homeland.

We dare not fail to see the insidious nature of this new and deeper struggle. We dare not fail to grasp the new concepts, the new tools, the new sense of urgency we will need to combat it-whether in Cuba or South Vietnam. And we dare not fail to realize that this struggle is taking place every day, without fanfare, in thousands of villages and markets-day and night-and in classrooms all over the globe.

The message of Cuba, of Laos, of the rising din of Communist voices in Asia and Latin America—these messages are all the same. The complacent, the self-indulgent, the soft societies are about to be swept away with the debris of history. Only the strong, only the industrious, only the determined; only the courageous, only the visionary who determines the real nature of our struggle can possibly survive.

No greater task faces this country or this administration. No other challenge is more deserving of our every effort and energy. Too long we have fixed our eyes on traditional military needs, on armies prepared to cross borders, on missiles poised for flight. Now it should be clear that this is no longer enough—that our security may be lost piece by piece, country by country, without the bring of a single missile or the crossing of a single border.

We intend to profit from this lesson. We intend to re-examine and reorient our forces of all kinds—our tactics and our institutions here in this community. We intend to intensify our efforts for a struggle in many ways more difficult than war, where disappointment will often accompany us.

For I am convinced that we, in this country and in the free world, possess the necessary resource and the skill, and the added strength that comes from a belief in the freedom of man. And I am equally convinced that history will record the fact that this bitter struggle reached its climax in the late 1950's and the early 1960's. Let me then make dear, as the President of the United States, that I am determined upon our system's survival and success, regardless of the cost and regardless of the peril!

Urban II

Most beloved brethren: Urged by necessity, I, Urban, by the permission of God, chief bishop, and prelate over the whole world have come into these parts as an ambassador with a divine admonition to you, the servants of God. I hoped to find you as faithful and as zealous in the service of God as I had supposed you to be. But if there is in you any deformity or crookedness contrary to God's law, with divine help, I will do my best to remove it. For God has put you as stewards over his family to minister to it. Happy, indeed, will you be if he finds you faithful in your stewardship.

You are called shepherds; see that you do not act as hirelings. But be true shepherds, with your crooks always in your hands.

Do not go to sleep, but guard on all sides the flock committed to you. For if through your carelessness or negligence a wolf carries away one of your sheep, you will surely lose the reward laid up for you with God.

And after you have been bitterly scourged with remorse for your faults, you will be fiercely overwhelmed in hell, the abode of death. For according to the gospel, you are the salt of the earth. But if you fall short in your duty, how, it may be asked, can it be salted? O how great the need of salting!

It is indeed necessary for you to correct, with the salt of wisdom, this foolish people, which is so devoted to the pleasures of this world, lest the Lord, when He may wish to speak to them, find them putrefied by their sins unsalted and stinking. For if He shall find worms, that is, sins, in them because you have been negligent in your duty, He will command them as worthless—to be thrown into the abyss of unclean things. And because you cannot restore to Him His great loss, He will surely condemn you and drive you from His loving presence. But the man who applies this salt should be prudent, provident, modest, learned, peaceable, watchful, pious, just, equitable, and pure.

For how can the ignorant teach others? How can the licentious make others modest?

And how can the impure make others pure? If anyone hates peace, how can he make others peaceable ? Or if anyone has soiled his hands with baseness, how can he cleanse the impurities of another?

We read also that if the blind lead the blind, both will fall into the ditch. But first correct yourselves, in order that, free from blame , you may be able to correct those who are subject to you. If you wish to be the friends of God, gladly do the things which you know will please Him.

16

You must especially let all matters that pertain to the church be controlled by the law of the church. And be careful that simony does not take root among you, lest both those who buy and those who sell be beaten with the scourges of the Lord, through narrow streets and driven into the place of destruction and confusion.

Keep the church and the clergy, in all its grades, entirely free from the secular power. See that the tithes that belong to God are faithfully paid from all the produce of the land; let them not be sold or withheld.

If anyone seizes a bishop, let him be treated as an outlaw. If anyone seizes or robs monks, or clergymen, or nuns, or their servants, or pilgrims, or merchants, let him be anathema. Let robbers, and incendiaries, and all their accomplices be expelled from the church and anathematized.

If a man who does not give a part of his goods as alms, is punished with the damnation of hell, how should he be punished who robs another of his goods? For thus it happened to the rich man in the gospel; he was not punished because he had stolen the goods of another, but because he had not used well the things which were his.

You have seen, for a long time, the great disorder in the world caused by these crimes. It is so bad in some of your provinces, I am told, and you are so weak in the administration of justice, that one can hardly go along the road by day or night without being attacked by robbers; and whether at home or abroad, one is in danger of being despoiled either by force or fraud.

Therefore, it is necessary to reenact the truce, as it is commonly called, which was proclaimed a long time ago by our holy fathers. I exhort and demand that you each try hard to have the truce kept in your diocese. And if anyone shall be led by his cupidity or arrogance to break this truce, by the authority of God and with the sanction of this council, he shall be anathematized.

Although, O sons of God, you have promised more firmly than ever to keep the peace among yourselves and to preserve the rights of the church, there remains still an important work for you to do. Freshly quickened by the divine correction, you must apply the strength of your righteousness to another matter which concerns you as well as God. For your brethren who live in the east, are in urgent need of your help, and you must hasten to give them the aid which has often been promised them.

For, as the most of you have heard, the Turks and Arabs have attacked them and have conquered the territory of Romania as far west as the shore of the Mediterranean and the Hellespont, which is called the Arm of St. George. They have occupied more and more of the lands of those Christians, and have overcome them in seven battles. They have killed and captured many, and have destroyed the churches and devastated the empire. If you permit them to continue thus for awhile with impurity, the faithful of God will be much more widely attacked by them.

On this account I or rather the Lord, beseech you as Christ's heralds to publish this everywhere and to persuade all people of whatever rank, foot-soldiers and knights, poor and rich, to carry aid promptly to those Christians and to destroy that vile race from the lands of our friends. I say this to those who are present, it is meant also for those who are absent. Moreover, Christ commands it.

All who die by the way, whether by land or by sea, or in battle against the pagans, shall have immediate remission of sins. This, I grant them through the power of God with which I am invested. O what a disgrace if such a despised and base race, which worships demons, should conquer a people which has the faith of omnipotent God and is made glorious with the name of Christ! With what reproaches will the Lord overwhelm us if you do not aid those who, with us, profess the Christian religion?

Let those who have been accustomed, unjustly, to wage private warfare against the faithful, now go against the infidels and end, with victory, this war which should have been begun long ago. Let those who for a long time, have been robbers, now become knights. Let those who have been fighting against their brothers and relatives now fight in a proper way against the barbarians.

Let those who have been serving as mercenaries for small pay now obtain the eternal reward. Let those who have been wearing themselves out in both body and soul now work for a double honor.

Behold! on this side will be the sorrowful and poor, on that, the rich; on this side, the enemies of the Lord; on that, his friends.

Let those who go, not put off the journey, but rent their lands and collect money for their expenses; and as soon as winter is over and spring comes, let them eagerly set out on the way with God as their guide.

John Hancock

Anniversary of the 1770 Boston Massacre
March 5, 1774

It was easy to foresee the consequences, which so naturally followed upon sending troops into America to enforce obedience to acts of the British Parliament, which neither God nor man ever empowered them to make. It was reasonable to expect that troops, who knew the errand they were sent upon, would treat the people whom they were to subjugate with a cruelty and haughtiness, which too often buried the honorable character of the soldier in the disgraceful name of an unfeeling ruffian.

The troops, upon their first arrival, took possession of our senate house and pointed their cannon against the judgment hall, and even continued them there whilst the supreme court of juridicature for this province was actually sitting to decide upon the lives and fortunes of the king's subjects.

Our streets nightly resounded with the noise of riot and debauchery; our peaceful citizens were hourly exposed to shameful insults and often felt the effects of their violence and outrage. But this was not all; as though they thought it not enough to violate our civil rights, they endeavored to deprive us of the enjoyment

21

of our religious privileges, to vitiate our morals and thereby render us deserving of destruction.

I come reluctantly to the transactions of that dismal night, when in such quick succession we felt the extremes of grief, astonishment, and rage; when Heaven in anger, for a dreadful moment, suffered hell to take the reins; when Satan, with his chosen band, opened the sluices of New England's blood and sacrilegiously polluted our land with the dead bodies of her guiltless sons.

Let this sad tale of death never be told without a tear; let not the heaving bosom cease to bum with a manly indignation at the barbarous story through the long tracts of future time; let every parent tell the shameful story to his listening children until tears of pity glisten in their eyes, and boiling passion shake their tender frames; and whilst the anniversary of that ill-fated night is kept a jubilee in the grim court of pandemonium, let all America join in one common prayer to Heaven, that the inhuman, unprovoked murders of the fifth of March, 1770, planned by Hillsborough and a knot of treacherous knaves in Boston, and executed by the cruel hand of Preston and his sanguinary coadjutors, may ever stand in history without parallel.

But what, my countrymen, withheld the ready arm of vengeance from executing instant justice on the vile assassins? May that magnificence of spirit which scorns the low pursuits of malice, may that generous compassion which often preserves from ruin, even a guilty villain, forever actuate the noble bosoms of Americans. But let not the miscreant host vainly imagine that we feared their arms. No, them we despised; we dread nothing but slavery. Death is the creature of a poltroon's brain; 'tis immortality to sacrifice ourselves for the salvation of our country.

We fear not death. That gloomy night, the pale-faced moon, and the affrighted stars that hurried through the sky can witness that we fear not death. Our hearts, which at the recollection, glow with rage that four revolving years have scarcely taught us to restrain, can witness that we fear not death; and happy it is for those who dared to insult us, that their naked bones are not now piled up an everlasting monument of Massachusetts' bravery.

Patrick Henry

Start of the American Revolution
March 23, 1775

Mr. President,

No man thinks more highly than I do of the patriotism, as well as abilities of the very worthy gentlemen who have just addressed the House. But different men often see the same subject in different lights; and, therefore, I hope that it will not be thought disrespectful to those gentlemen, if, entertaining as I do, opinions of a character very opposite to theirs, I shall speak forth my sentiments freely and without reserve. This is no time for ceremony.

The question before the House is one of awful moment to this country. For my own part, I consider it as nothing less than a question of freedom or slavery; and in proportion to the magnitude of the subject ought to be the freedom of the debate. It is only in this way that we can hope to arrive at truth, and fulfill the great responsibility, which we hold to God and our country.

Should I keep back my opinions at such a time, through fear of giving offence, I should consider myself as guilty of treason towards my country, and of an act of disloyalty towards the majesty of heaven, which I revere above all earthly kings.

Mr. President, it is natural to man to indulge in the illusions of hope. We are apt to shut our eyes against a painful truth, and listen to the song of that siren, till she transforms us into beasts. Is this the part of wise men, engaged in a great and arduous struggle for liberty?

Are we disposed to be of the number of those who, having eyes, see not, and having ears, hear not, the things which so nearly concern their temporal salvation?

For my part, for whatever anguish of spirit it may cost, I am willing to know the whole truth; to know the worst and to provide for it. I have but one lamp by which my feet are guided; and that is the lamp of experience. I know of no way of judging of the future but by the past. And judging by the past, I wish to know what there has been, in the conduct of the British ministry for the last ten years, to justify those hopes with which gentlemen have been pleased to solace themselves and the House. Is it that insidious smile with which our petition has been lately received?

Trust it not, sir; it will prove a snare to your feet. Suffer not yourselves to be betrayed with a kiss. Ask yourselves how this gracious reception of our petition comports with these war-like preparations which cover our waters and darken our land. Are fleets and armies necessary to a work of love and reconciliation? Have we shown ourselves so unwilling to be reconciled, that force must be called in to win back our love? Let us not deceive ourselves, sir. These are the implements of war and subjugation; the last arguments to which kings resort.

I ask gentlemen, sir, what means this martial array, if its purpose be not to force us to submission? Can gentlemen assign any other possible motives for it? Has Great Britain any enemy, in this quarter of the world, to call for all this accumulation of navies and armies?

No, sir, she has none. They are meant for us; they can be meant for no other. They are sent over to bind and rivet upon us those chains, which the British ministry have been so long forging.

And what have we to oppose to them? Shall we try argument? Sir, we have been trying that for the last ten years. Have we anything new to offer on the subject? Nothing!

We have held the subject up in every light of which it is capable; but it has been all in vain. Shall we resort to entreaty and humble supplication? What terms shall we find which have not been already exhausted? Let us not, I beseech you, sir, deceive ourselves longer.

Sir, we have done everything that could be done to avert the storm, which is now coming on. We have

26

petitioned; we have remonstrated; we have supplicated; we have prostrated ourselves before the throne, and have implored its interposition to arrest the tyrannical hands of the ministry and Parliament.

Our petitions have been slighted; our remonstrances have produced additional violence and insult; our supplications have been disregarded; and we have been spurned, with contempt, from the foot of the throne. In vain, after these things, may we indulge the fond hope of peace and reconciliation.

There is no longer any room for hope. If we wish to be free—if we mean to preserve inviolate those inestimable privileges for which we have been so long contending—if we mean not basely to abandon the noble struggle in which we have been so long engaged, and which we have pledged ourselves never to abandon until the glorious object of our contest shall be obtained, we must fight! I repeat it, sir, we must fight!

An appeal to arms and to the God of Hosts is all that is left us!

They tell us, sir, that we are weak—unable to cope with so formidable an adversary. But when shall we be stronger? Will it be the next week or the next year? Will it be when we are totally disarmed, and when a British guard shall be stationed in every house? Shall we gather strength by irresolution and inaction? Shall we acquire the means of effectual resistance, by lying supinely on our backs and hugging the delusive phantom of hope until our enemies shall have bound us hand and foot?

Sir, we are not weak if we make proper use of the means, which the God of nature hath placed in our power. Three millions of people, armed in the holy cause of liberty, and in such a country as that which we possess, are invincible by any force which our enemy can send against us. Besides, sir, we shall not fight our battles alone.

There is a just God who presides over the destinies of nations, and who will raise up friends to fight our battles for us. The battle, sir, is not to the strong alone; it is to the vigilant, the active, the brave. Besides, sir, we have no election. If we were base enough to desire it, it is now too late to retire from the contest.

There is no retreat, but in submission and slavery!

Our chains are forged. Their clanking may be heard on the plains of Boston. The war is inevitable—and let it come! I repeat it, sir, let it come!

It is in vain, sir, to extenuate the matter. Gentlemen may cry peace, peace—but there is no peace. The war is actually begun.

The next gale that sweeps from the north will bring to our ears the clash of resounding arms. Our brethren are already in the field. Why stand we here idle? What is it that gentlemen wish? What would they have? Is life so dear, or peace so sweet, as to be purchased at the price of chains and slavery?

Forbid it, Almighty God! I know not what course others may take; but as for me, give me liberty, or give me death!

Thomas Paine

Excerpts from *Common Sense*
1776

Volumes have been written on the subject of the struggle between England and America. Men of all ranks have embarked in the controversy, from different motives and with various designs; but all have been ineffectual and the period of debate is closed. Arms, as the last resource, decide the contest; the appeal was the choice of the king, and the continent hath accepted the challenge.

Whatever was advanced by the advocates on either side of the question then, terminated in one and the same point, a union with Great Britain; the only difference between the parties was the method of effecting it; the one proposing force, the other friendship; but it hath so far happened that the first hath failed, and the second hath withdrawn her influence.

We have boasted the protection of Great Britain, without considering, that her motive was interest not attachment; that she did not protect us from our enemies on our account but from her enemies on her own account, from those who had no quarrel with us on any other account, and who will always be our enemies on the same account. Let Britain wave her pretensions to the continent, or the continent throw off the dependence, and we should be at peace with France and Spain were they at war with Britain.

In this extensive quarter of the globe, we forget the narrow limits of three hundred and sixty miles (the extent of England) and carry our friendship on a larger scale; we claim brotherhood with every European Christian, and triumph in the generosity of the sentiment.

But admitting that we were all of English descent, what does it amount to? Nothing. Britain, being now an open enemy, extinguishes every other name and title: And to say that reconciliation is our duty is truly farcical. The first king of England, of the present line (William the Conqueror) was a Frenchman, and half the peers of England are descendants from the same country; wherefore by the same method of reasoning, England ought to be governed by France.

Much hath been said of the united strength of Britain and the colonies, that in conjunction they might bid defiance to the world. But this is mere presumption; the fate of war is uncertain. Neither do the expressions mean anything; for this continent would never suffer itself to be drained of inhabitants to support the British arms in either Asia, Africa, or Europe.

Besides, what have we to do with setting the world at defiance? Our plan is commerce, and that, well attended to, will secure us the peace and friendship of all Europe; because it is the interest of all Europe to have America a free port. Her trade will always be a protection, and her barrenness of gold and silver secure her from invaders.

I challenge the warmest advocate for reconciliation, to show, a single advantage that this continent can reap by being connected with Great Britain. I repeat the challenge; not a single advantage is derived. Our corn will fetch its price in any market in Europe, and our imported goods must be paid for—buy them where we will.

But the injuries and disadvantages we sustain by that connection are without number; and our duty to mankind I at large, as well as to ourselves, instruct us to renounce the alliance: Because, any submission to, or dependence on Great Britain, tends directly to involve this continent in European wars and quarrels; and sets us at variance with nations, who would otherwise seek our friendship, and against whom, we have neither anger nor complaint.

As Europe is our market for trade, we ought to form no partial connection with any part of it. It is the true interest of America to steer clear of European contentions, which she never can do, while by her dependence on Britain, she is made the make-weight in the scale of British politics.

The authority of Great Britain over this continent, is a form of government, which sooner or later must have an end: And a serious mind can draw no true pleasure by looking forward, under the painful and positive conviction, that what he calls "the present constitution" is merely temporary.

Men of passive tempers look somewhat lightly over the offenses of Britain, and, still hoping for the best, are apt to call out, "Come we shall be friends again for all this."

But examine the passions and feelings of mankind. Bring the doctrine of reconciliation to the touchstone of nature, and then tell me, whether you can hereafter love, honor, and faithfully serve the power that hath carried fire and sword into your land? If you cannot do all these, then are you only deceiving yourselves, and by your delay, bringing ruin upon posterity.

Your future connection with Britain, whom you can neither love nor honor, will be forced and unnatural, and being formed only on the plan of present convenience, will in a little time, fall into a relapse more wretched than the first

Every quiet method for peace hath been ineffectual. Our prayers have been rejected with disdain; and only tended to convince us that nothing flatters vanity or confirms obstinacy in kings more than repeated petitioning—and nothing hath contributed more than that very measure to make the kings of Europe absolute: Witness Denmark and Sweden. Wherefore since nothing but blows will do, for God's sake, let us come to a final separation and not leave the next generation to be cutting throats under the violated unmeaning names of parent and child.

As to government matters, it is not in the powers of Britain to do this continent justice: The business of it will soon be too weighty and intricate to be managed with any tolerable degree of convenience by a power so distant from us and so very ignorant of us; for if they cannot conquer us, they cannot govern us.

To be always running three or four thousand miles with a tale or a petition, waiting four or five months for an answer, which when obtained requires five or six more to explain it in, will in a few years be looked upon as folly and childishness. There was a time when it was proper, and there is a proper time for it to cease.

Small islands not capable of protecting themselves are the proper objects for kingdoms to take under their care; but there is something very absurd in supposing a continent to be perpetually governed by an island. In no instance hath nature made the satellite larger than its primary planet, and as England and America, with respect to each Other, reverses the common order of nature, it is evident they belong to different systems: England to Europe—America to itself.

George H.W. Bush

Invasion of Iraq: Operation Desert Storm
Jan 16, 1991

Just 2 hours ago, allied air forces began an attack on military targets in Iraq and Kuwait. These attacks continue as I speak. Ground forces are not engaged.

This conflict started August 2nd when the dictator of Iraq invaded a small and helpless neighbor. Kuwait—a member of the Arab League and a member of the United Nations—was crushed; its people brutalized. Five months ago, Saddam Hussein started this cruel war against Kuwait. Tonight, the battle has been joined.

This military action, taken in accord with United Nations resolutions and with the consent of the United States Congress, follows months of constant and virtually endless diplomatic activity on the part of the United Nations, the United States, and many, many other countries. Arab leaders sought what became known as an Arab solution, only to conclude that Saddam Hussein was unwilling to leave Kuwait.

Others traveled to Baghdad in a variety of efforts to restore peace and justice. Our Secretary of State, James Baker, held an historic meeting in Geneva, only to be totally rebuffed. This past weekend, in a last-ditch effort, the Secretary-General of the United Nations went to the Middle East with peace in his heart—his second such mission. And he came back from Baghdad with no progress at all in getting Saddam Hussein to withdraw from Kuwait.

Now the 28 countries, with forces in the Gulf area, have exhausted all reasonable efforts to reach a peaceful resolution—have no choice but to drive Saddam from Kuwait by force. We will not fail.

As I report to you, air attacks are underway against military targets in Iraq. We are determined to knock out Saddam Hussein's nuclear bomb potential. We will also destroy his chemical weapons facilities. Much of Saddam's artillery and tanks will be destroyed. Our operations are designed to best protect the lives of all the coalition forces by targeting Saddam's vast military arsenal. Initial reports from General Schwarzkopf are that our operations are proceeding according to plan.

Our objectives are clear: Saddam Hussein's forces will leave Kuwait. The legitimate government of Kuwait will be restored to its rightful place and Kuwait will once again be free. Iraq will eventually comply with all relevant United Nations resolutions, and then, when peace is restored, it is our hope that Iraq will live as a peaceful and cooperative member of the family of nations, thus enhancing the security and stability of the Gulf.

Some may ask: Why act now? Why not wait? The answer is clear: The world could wait no longer.

Sanctions, though having some effect, showed no signs of accomplishing their objective. Sanctions were tried for well over 5 months, and we and our allies concluded that sanctions alone would not force Saddam from Kuwait.

While the world waited, Saddam Hussein systematically raped, pillaged, and plundered a tiny nation, no threat to his own. He subjected the people of Kuwait to unspeakable atrocities—and among those, maimed and murdered innocent children.

While the world waited, Saddam sought to add to the chemical weapons arsenal he now possesses, an infinitely more dangerous weapon of mass destruction—a nuclear weapon. And while the world waited, while the world talked peace and withdrawal, Saddam Hussein dug in and moved massive forces into Kuwait.

While the world waited, while Saddam stalled, more damage was being done to the fragile economies of the Third World, emerging democracies of Eastern Europe, to the entire world, including to our own economy.

The United States, together with the United Nations, exhausted every means at our disposal to bring this crisis to a peaceful end. However, Saddam clearly felt that by stalling and threatening and defying the United Nations, he could weaken the forces arrayed against him.

While the world waited, Saddam Hussein met every overture of peace with open contempt. While the world prayed for peace, Saddam prepared for war.

I had hoped that when the United States Congress, in historic debate, took its resolute action, Saddam would realize he could not prevail and would move out of Kuwait in accord with the United Nation resolutions. He did not do that. Instead, he remained intransigent, certain that time was on his side.

Saddam was warned over and over again to comply with the will of the United Nations: Leave Kuwait, or be driven out. Saddam has arrogantly rejected all warnings. Instead, he tried to make this a dispute between Iraq and the United States of America.

Well, he failed. Tonight, 28 nations—countries from 5 continents, Europe and Asia, Africa, and the Arab League—have forces in the Gulf area standing shoulder to shoulder against Saddam Hussein. These countries had hoped the use of force could be avoided. Regrettably, we now believe that only force will make him leave.

Prior to ordering our forces into battle, I instructed our military commanders to take every necessary step to prevail as quickly as possible, and with the greatest degree of protection possible for American and allied service men and women. I've told the American people before that this will not be another Vietnam, and I repeat this here tonight. Our troops will have the best possible support in the entire world, and they will not be asked to fight with one hand tied behind their back. I'm hopeful that this fighting will not go on for long and that casualties will be held to an absolute minimum.

This is an historic moment. We have in this past year made great progress in ending the long era of conflict and cold war. We have before us the opportunity to forge for ourselves and for future generations a new world order—a world where the rule of law, not the law of the jungle, governs the conduct of nations. When we are successful—and we will be—we have a real chance at this new world order, an order in which a credible United Nations can use its peacekeeping role to fulfill the promise and vision of the U.N.'s founders.

We have no argument with the people of Iraq. Indeed, for the innocents caught in this conflict, I pray for their safety. Our goal is not the conquest of Iraq. It is the liberation of Kuwait. It is my hope that somehow the Iraqi people can, even now, convince their dictator that he must lay down his arms, leave Kuwait, and let Iraq itself rejoin the family of peace-loving nations.

Thomas Paine wrote many years ago: "These are the times that try men's souls."

Those well-known words are so very true today. But even as planes of the multinational forces attack Iraq, I prefer to think of peace, not war. I am convinced not only that we will prevail but that out of the horror of

39

combat will come the recognition that no nation can stand against a world united, no nation will be permitted to brutally assault its neighbor.

No President can easily commit our sons and daughters to war. They are the Nation's finest. Ours is an all-volunteer force, magnificently trained, highly motivated. The troops know why they're there. And listen to what they say, for they've said it better than any President or Prime Minister ever could.

Listen to Hollywood Huddleston, Marine lance corporal. He says, "Let's free these people, so we can go home and be free again." And he's right. The terrible crimes and tortures committed by Saddam's henchmen against the innocent people of Kuwait are an affront to mankind and a challenge to the freedom of all.

Listen to one of our great officers out there, Marine Lieutenant General Walter Boomer. He said: "There are things worth fighting for. A world in which brutality and lawlessness are allowed to go unchecked isn't the kind of world we're going to want to live in."

Listen to Master Sergeant J.P. Kendall of the 82nd Airborne: "We're here for more than just the price of a gallon of gas. What we're doing is going to chart the future of the world for the next 100 years. It's better to deal with this guy now than 5 years from now."

40

And finally, we should all sit up and listen to Jackie Jones, an Army lieutenant, when she says, "If we let him get away with this, who knows what's going to be next?"

I have called upon Hollywood and Walter and J.P. and Jackie and all their courageous comrades-in-arms to do what must be done. Tonight, America and the world are deeply grateful to them and to their families. And let me say to everyone listening or watching tonight: When the troops we've sent in finish their work, I am determined to bring them home as soon as possible.

Tonight, as our forces fight, they and their families are in our prayers. May God bless each and every one of them, and the coalition forces at our side in the Gulf, and may He continue to bless our nation, the United States of America.

41

Lyndon Baines Johnson

Not Seeking Re-election
March 31, 1968

Good evening, my fellow Americans:

Tonight I want to speak to you of peace in Vietnam and Southeast Asia. No other question so preoccupies our people. No other dream so absorbs the 250 million human beings who live in that part of the world. No other goal motivates American policy in Southeast Asia.

For years, representatives of our Governments and others have traveled the world seeking to find a basis for peace talks. Since last September they have carried the offer that I made public at San Antonio. And that offer was this:

That the United States would stop its bombardment of North Vietnam when that would lead promptly to productive discussions—and that we would assume that North Vietnam would not take military advantage of our restraint.

Hanoi denounced this offer, both privately and publicly. Even while the search for peace was going on, North Vietnam rushed their preparations for a savage assault on the people, the government, and the allies of South Vietnam. Their attack—during the Tet

42

holidays—failed to achieve its principal objectives. It did not collapse the elected Government of South Vietnam or shatter its army—as the Communists had hoped. It did not produce a "general uprising" among the people of the cities, as they had predicted. The Communists were unable to maintain control of any of the more than 30 cities that they attacked. And they took very heavy casualties. But they did compel the South Vietnamese and their allies to move certain forces from the countryside into the cities. They caused widespread disruption and suffering. Their attacks, and the battles that followed, made refugees of half a million human beings.

The Communists may renew their attack any day. They are, it appears, trying to make 1968 the year of decision in South Vietnam—the year that brings, if not final victory or defeat, at least a turning point in the struggle.

This much is clear: If they do mount another round of heavy attacks, they will not succeed in destroying the fighting power of South Vietnam and its allies. But tragically, this is also clear: Many men, on both sides of the struggle, will be lost. A nation that has already suffered 20 years of warfare will suffer once again. Armies on both sides will take new casualties. And the war will go on. There is no need for this to be so. There is no need to delay the talks that could bring an end to this long and this bloody war.

Tonight, I renew the offer I made last August: to stop the bombardment of North Vietnam. We ask that talks begin promptly, that they be serious talks on the substance of peace. We assume that during those talks Hanoi will not take advantage of our restraint. We are prepared to move immediately toward peace through negotiations. So tonight, in the hope that this action will lead to early talks, I am taking the first step to de-escalate the conflict. We are reducing—substantially reducing—the present level of hostilities, and we are doing so unilaterally and at once.

Tonight, I have ordered our aircraft and our naval vessels to make no attacks on North Vietnam, except in the area north of the demilitarized zone where the continuing enemy buildup directly threatens allied forward positions and where the movements of their troops and supplies are clearly related to that threat. The area in which we are stopping our attacks includes almost 90 percent of North Vietnam's population and most of its territory. Thus, there will be no attacks around the principal populated areas, or in the food-producing areas of North Vietnam.

Even this very limited bombing of the North could come to an early end if our restraint is matched by restraint in Hanoi. But I cannot in good conscience stop all bombing so long as to do so would immediately and directly endanger the lives of our men and our allies. Whether a complete bombing halt becomes possible in the future will be determined by events.

Our purpose in this action is to bring about a reduction in the level of violence that now exists. It is to save the lives of brave men—and to save the lives of innocent women and children. It is to permit the contending forces to move closer to a political settlement. And tonight I call upon the United Kingdom and I call upon the Soviet Union—as co-chairmen of the Geneva conferences and as permanent members of the United Nations Security Council—to do all they can to move from the unilateral act of de-escalation that I have just announced toward genuine peace in Southeast Asia.

Now, as in the past, the United States is ready to send its representatives to any forum, at any time, to discuss the means of bringing this ugly war to an end. I am designating one of our most distinguished Americans, Ambassador Averell Harriman, as my personal representative for such talks. In addition, I have asked Ambassador Llewellyn Thompson, who returned from Moscow for consultation, to be available to join Ambassador Harriman at Geneva or any other suitable place—just as soon as Hanoi agrees to a conference.

I call upon President Ho Chi Minh to respond positively and favorably to this new step toward peace. But if peace does not come now through negotiations, it will come when Hanoi understands that our common resolve is unshakable and our common strength is invincible.

Tonight, we and the other allied nations are contributing 600,000 fighting men to assist 700,000 South Vietnamese troops in defending their little country. Our presence there has always rested on this basic belief: The main burden of preserving their freedom must be carried out by them—by the South Vietnamese themselves.

We and our allies can only help to provide a shield behind which the people of South Vietnam can survive and can grow and develop. On their efforts—on their determinations and resourcefulness—the outcome will ultimately depend. That small, beleaguered nation has suffered terrible punishment for more than 20 years. I pay tribute once again tonight to the great courage and the endurance of its people. South Vietnam supports armed forces tonight of almost 700,000 men, and I call your attention to the fact that that is the equivalent of more than 10 million in our own population. Its people maintain their firm determination to be free of domination by the North.

There has been substantial progress, I think, in building a durable government during these last three years. The South Vietnam of 1965 could not have survived the enemy's Tet offensive of 1968. The elected government of South Vietnam survived that attack—and is rapidly repairing the devastation that it wrought. The South Vietnamese know that further efforts are going to be required to expand their own armed forces; to move back into the countryside as quickly as possible; to increase their taxes; to select the very best men that they have for civil and military responsibilities; to achieve a new unity within their constitutional government, and to include in the national effort all those groups who wish to preserve South Vietnam's control over its own destiny.

Last week, President Thieu ordered the mobilization of 135,000 additional South Vietnamese. He plans to reach, as soon as possible, a total military strength of more than 800,000 men. To achieve this, the Government of South Vietnam started the drafting of 19-year-olds on March 1st. On May 1st, the Government will begin the drafting of 18-year-olds. Last month, 10,000 men volunteered for military service. That was two and a half times the number of volunteers during the same month last year. Since the middle of January, more than 48,000 South Vietnamese have joined the armed forces, and nearly half of them volunteered to do so.

All men in the South Vietnamese armed forces have had their tours of duty extended for the duration of the war, and reserves are now being called up for immediate active duty. President Thieu told his people last week, and I quote:

"We must make greater efforts, we must accept more sacrifices, because as I have said many times, this is our country. The existence of our nation is at stake, and this is mainly a Vietnamese responsibility."

He warned his people that a major national effort is required to root out corruption and incompetence at all levels of government. We applaud this evidence of determination on the part of South Vietnam. Our first priority will be to support their effort. We shall accelerate the re-equipment of South Vietnam's armed forces in order to meet the enemy's increased firepower. And this will enable them progressively to undertake a larger share of combat operations against the Communist invaders.

On many occasions I have told the American people that we would send to Vietnam those forces that are required to accomplish our mission there. So with that as our guide we have previously authorized a force level of approximately 525,000. Some weeks ago to help meet the enemy's new offensive we sent to Vietnam about 11,000 additional Marine and airborne troops. They were deployed by air in 48 hours on an emergency basis. But the artillery and the tank and the aircraft and medical and other units that were needed to work with and support these infantry troops in combat could not then accompany them by air on that short notice.

In order that these forces may reach maximum combat effectiveness, the Joint Chiefs of Staff have recommended to me that we should prepare to send during the next five months the support troops totaling approximately 13,500 men. A portion of these men will be made available from our active forces. The balance will come from reserve component units, which will be called up for service.

The actions that we have taken since the beginning of the year to re-equip the South Vietnamese forces to meet our responsibilities in Korea, as well as our responsibilities in Vietnam, to meet price increases and the cost of activating and deploying these reserve forces, to replace helicopters and provide the other military supplies we need—all of these actions are going to require additional expenditures.

The tentative estimate of those additional expenditures is 2 1/2 billion dollars in this fiscal year and 2 billion, 600 million in the next fiscal year. These projected increases in expenditures for our national security will bring into sharper focus the nation's need for immediate action, action to protect the prosperity of the American people and to protect the strength and the stability of our American dollar.

On many occasions I have pointed out that without a tax bill or decreased expenditures, next year's deficit would again be around $20 billion. I have emphasized the need to set strict priorities in our spending. I have stressed that failure to act—and to act promptly and decisively—would raise very strong doubts throughout the world about America's willingness to keep its financial house in order.

Yet Congress has not acted. And tonight we face the sharpest financial threat in the postwar era—a threat to the dollar's role as the keystone of international trade and finance in the world.

Last week, at the monetary conference in Stockholm, the major industrial countries decided to take a big step toward creating a new international monetary asset that will strengthen the international monetary system. And I'm very proud of the very able work done by Secretary Fowler and Chairman Martin of the Federal Reserve Board. But to make this system work, the United States just must bring its balance of payments to—or very close to—equilibrium. We must have a responsible fiscal policy in this country. The passage of a tax bill now, together with expenditure control that the Congress may desire and dictate, is absolutely necessary to protect this nation's security, and to continue our prosperity, and to meet the needs of our people.

Now, what is at stake is seven years of unparalleled prosperity. In those seven years, the real income of the average American, after taxes, rose by almost 30 percent—a gain as large as that of the entire preceding 19 years. So the steps that we must take to convince the world are exactly the steps that we must take to sustain our own economic strength here at home. In the past eight months, prices and interest rates have risen because of our inaction. We must therefore now do everything we can to move from debate to action, from talking to voting, and there is, I believe—I hope there is—in both Houses of the Congress, a growing sense of urgency that this situation just must be acted upon and must be corrected.

My budget in January, we thought, was a tight one. It fully reflected our evaluation of most of the demanding needs of this nation. But in these budgetary matters, the President does not decide alone. The Congress has the power and the duty to determine appropriations and taxes. And the Congress is now considering our proposals, and they are considering reductions in the budget that we submitted.

As part of a program of fiscal restraint that includes the tax surcharge, I shall approve appropriate reductions in the January budget when and if Congress so decides that that should be done. One thing is unmistakably clear, however. Our deficit just must be reduced. Failure to act could bring on conditions that would strike hardest at those people that all of us are trying so hard to help

So these times call for prudence in this land of plenty. And I believe that we have the character to provide it, and tonight I plead with the Congress and with the people to act promptly to serve the national interest and thereby serve all of our people.

Now let me give you my estimate of the chances for peace—the peace that will one day stop the bloodshed in South Vietnam; that will—all the Vietnamese people [will] be permitted to rebuild and develop their land;

51

that will permit us to turn more fully to our own tasks here at home. I cannot promise that the initiative that I have announced tonight will be completely successful in achieving peace any more than the 30 others that we have undertaken and agreed to in recent years. But it is our fervent hope that North Vietnam, after years of fighting that has left the issue unresolved, will now cease its efforts to achieve a military victory and will join with us in moving toward the peace table.

And there may come a time when South Vietnamese— on both sides—are able to work out a way to settle their own differences by free political choice rather than by war. As Hanoi considers its course, it should be in no doubt of our intentions. It must not miscalculate the pressures within our democracy in this election year. We have no intention of widening this war. But the United States will never accept a fake solution to this long and arduous struggle and call it peace.

No one can foretell the precise terms of an eventual settlement. Our objective in South Vietnam has never been the annihilation of the enemy. It has been to bring about a recognition in Hanoi that its objective— taking over the South by force—could not be achieved. We think that peace can be based on the Geneva Accords of 1954, under political conditions that permit the South Vietnamese—all the South Vietnamese—to chart their course free of any outside domination or interference, from us or from anyone else.

52

So tonight, I reaffirm the pledge that we made at Manila: that we are prepared to withdraw our forces from South Vietnam as the other side withdraws its forces to the North, stops the infiltration, and the level of violence thus subsides. Our goal of peace and self-determination in Vietnam is directly related to the future of all of Southeast Asia, where much has happened to inspire confidence during the past 10 years. And we have done all that we knew how to do to contribute and to help build that confidence.

A number of its nations have shown what can be accomplished under conditions of security. Since 1966, Indonesia, the fifth largest nation in all the world, with a population of more than 100 million people, has had a government that's dedicated to peace with its neighbors and improved conditions for its own people.

Political and economic cooperation between nations has grown rapidly. And I think every American can take a great deal of pride in the role that we have played in bringing this about in Southeast Asia. We can rightly judge—as responsible Southeast Asians themselves do—that the progress of the past three years would have been far less likely, if not completely impossible, if America's sons and others had not made their stand in Vietnam.

At Johns Hopkins University about three years ago, I announced that the United States would take part in the great work of developing Southeast Asia, including the Mekong valley, for all the people of that region.

Our determination to help build a better land—a better land for men on both sides of the present conflict—has not diminished in the least. Indeed, the ravages of war, I think, have made it more urgent than ever.

So I repeat on behalf of the United States again tonight what I said at Johns Hopkins—that North Vietnam could take its place in this common effort just as soon as peace comes. Over time, a wider framework of peace and security in Southeast Asia may become possible. The new co-operations of the nations of the area could be a foundation stone. Certainly friendship with the nations of such a Southeast Asia is what the United States seeks—and that is all that the United States seeks.

One day, my fellow citizen, there will be peace in Southeast Asia. It will come because the people of Southeast Asia want it—those whose armies are at war tonight—those who, though threatened, have thus far been spared. Peace will come because Asians were willing to work for it and to sacrifice for it—and to die by the thousands for it. But let it never be forgotten: peace will come also because America sent her sons to help secure it.

It has not been easy—far from it. During the past four and a half years, it has been my fate and my responsibility to be Commander in Chief. I have lived daily and nightly with the cost of this war. I know the pain that it has inflicted. I know perhaps better than anyone the misgivings that it has aroused. And throughout this entire long period I have been sustained by a single principle: that what we are doing now in Vietnam is vital not only to the security of Southeast Asia, but it is vital to the security of every American.

Surely, we have treaties which we must respect. Surely, we have commitments that we are going to keep. Resolutions of the Congress testify to the need to resist aggression in the world and in Southeast Asia.

But the heart of our involvement in South Vietnam under three different presidents, three separate Administrations, has always been America's own security. And the larger purpose of our involvement has always been to help the nations of Southeast Asia become independent, and stand alone, self-sustaining as members of a great world community, at peace with themselves, at peace with all others. And with such a nation, our country and the world will be far more secure than it is tonight.

I believe that a peaceful Asia is far nearer to reality because of what America has done in Vietnam. I believe that the men who endure the dangers of battle there, fighting there for us tonight, are helping the entire world avoid far greater conflicts, far wider wars, far more destruction, than this one. The peace that will bring them home someday will come. Tonight, I have offered the first in what I hope will be a series of mutual moves toward peace.

I pray that it will not be rejected by the leaders of North Vietnam. I pray that they will accept it as a means by which the sacrifices of their own people may be ended. And I ask your help and your support, my fellow citizens, for this effort to reach across the battlefield toward an early peace.

Finally, my fellow Americans, let me say this: Of those to whom much is given, much is asked. I cannot say—and no man could say—that no more will be asked of us. Yet I believe that now, no less than when the decade began, this "generation of Americans" is willing to "pay any price, bear any burden, meet any hardship, support any friend, oppose any foe to assure the survival and the success of liberty."

Since those words were spoken by John F. Kennedy, the people of America have kept that compact with mankind's noblest cause. And we shall continue to keep it.

Yet, I believe that we must always be mindful of this one thing—whatever the trials and the tests ahead, the ultimate strength of our country and our cause will lie, not in powerful weapons or infinite resources or boundless wealth, but will lie in the unity of our people.

This I believe very deeply. Throughout my entire public career I have followed the personal philosophy that I am a free man, an American, a public servant, and a member of my party—in that order—always and only.

For 37 years in the service of our nation, first as a Congressman, as a Senator, and as Vice President, and now as your President, I have put the unity of the people first. I have put it ahead of any divisive partisanship. And in these times as in times before, it is true that a house divided against itself by the spirit of faction, of party, of region, of religion, of race—is a house that cannot stand.

There is division in the American house now. There is divisiveness among us all tonight. And holding the trust that is mine, as President of all the people, I cannot disregard the peril to the progress of the American people and the hope and the prospects of peace for all peoples. So, I would ask all Americans, whatever their personal interests or concern, to guard against divisiveness and all of its ugly consequences.

Fifty-two months and ten days ago, in a moment of tragedy and trauma, the duties of this office fell upon me. I asked then for your help and God's, that we might continue America on its course, binding up our wounds, healing our history, moving forward in new unity to clear the American agenda and to keep the American commitment for all of our people.

United we have kept that commitment. And united we have enlarged that commitment. And through all time to come I think America will be a stronger nation, a more just society, a land of greater opportunity and fulfillment because of what we have all done together in these years of unparalleled achievement.

Our reward will come in the life of freedom and peace and hope that our children will enjoy through ages ahead. What we won when all of our people united just must not now be lost in suspicion and distrust and selfishness and politics among any of our people. And believing this, as I do, I have concluded that I should not permit the Presidency to become involved in the partisan divisions that are developing in this political year.

With American sons in the fields far away, with America's future under challenge right here at home, with our hopes and the world's hopes for peace in the balance every day, I do not believe that I should devote an hour or a day of my time to any personal partisan causes or to any duties other than the awesome duties of this office—the Presidency of your country.

Accordingly, I shall not seek and I will not accept, the nomination of my party for another term as your President. But let men everywhere know, however, that a strong and a confident and a vigilant America stands ready tonight to seek an honorable peace—and stands ready tonight to defend an honored cause, whatever the price, whatever the burden, whatever the sacrifice that duty may require.

Thank you for listening. Good night and God bless all of you.

Golda Meir

Attainment of Peace between Egypt and Israel
May 26, 1970

We must view recent happenings against the whole background of our struggle, since the Six-Day War, to realize Israel's highest aspiration, the aspiration to peace.

To our intense disappointment, we learned on the morrow of the Six-Day War that the rulers of the Arab States and the Soviet Union were not prepared to put an end to the conflict. Witness authoritative fulminations by the Arab Governments, the resolutions of Khartoum, the Soviet Union's identification with that policy, its assiduous efforts to rehabilitate the Arab armies with lavish and unstinted aid.

We learned that our struggle for peace would be prolonged, full of pain and sacrifice. We decided—and the nation was with us—resolutely to defend the cease-fire lines against all aggression and simultaneously press on with our strivings to attain peace.

It is our way not to glorify ourselves but to render a sober and restrained account of our policy, not hiding the hard truth from the people, even if it be grievous. The people and the world know that there is no word of truth in Egypt's fabrication of resounding victories.

The main efforts of the Egyptian army have been repelled by the Israel Defense Forces. All claims of success in breaking our line are false. Most attempted sorties by Egyptian planes into our air-space have been undone, and the Egyptians are paying a heavy price for every venture to clash with our Air Force. We control the area all along the Canal cease-fire line more firmly and strongly than ever.

Three years after the Six-Day War, we can affirm that two fundamental principles have become a permanent part of the international consciousness: Israel's right to stand fast on the cease-fire lines, not budging until the conclusion of peace that will fix secure and recognized boundaries, and its right to self-defense and to acquire the equipment essential to defense and deterrence.

I have, on several occasions, explained the differences in appraisal and approach between ourselves and friendly States and Powers. I have no intention of claiming that they have entirely disappeared. Nevertheless, we cannot allow them to overshadow the recognition of those twin principles, any more than we may overlook the systematic plotting of our enemies to weaken that international consciousness and isolate Israel...

On 1 March 1957, in the name of the Government of Israel, I announced in the United Nations the withdrawal of our forces from the territories occupied in the Sinai Campaign. I concluded with these words:

Can we, from now on—all of us—turn over a new leaf, and instead of fighting with each other, can we all, united, fight poverty and disease and illiteracy? Is it possible for us to put all our efforts and all our energy into one single purpose, the betterment and progress and development of all our lands and all our peoples?

I can here pledge the Government and the people of Israel to do their part in this united effort. There is no limit to what we are prepared to contribute so that all of us, together, can live to see a day of happiness for our peoples and see again a great contribution from our region to peace and happiness for all humanity.

Ten years went by, of fedayun activity, and once again we were confronted with the hazard of a surprise attack by Egypt, which had assembled powerful columns in eastern Sinai. The Six-Day War was fought, but when its battles ended, we did not behave as men drunk with victory, we did not call for vengeance, we did not demand the humiliation of the conquered. We knew that our real celebration would be on the day that peace comes. Instantly, we turned to our neighbors, saying:

Our region is now at a crossroads: let us sit down together, not as victors and conquered, but as equals; let us negotiate, let us determine secure and agreed boundaries, let us write a new page of peace, good-neighborliness, and cooperation for the profit of all the nations of the Middle East.

61

The call was sounded over and again in Government statements, in declarations by the Prime Minister, the Deputy Prime Minister, the Foreign Minister, the Minister of Defense, and other Ministers—in the Knesset and in the United Nations, through all communication media. It was borne by emissaries, statesmen, authors, journalists, educators, and by every means—public or covert—which seemed likely to bring it to our neighbors' ears.

The Knesset will not expect me to review the manifold efforts and attempts to establish any kind of contact with statesmen and competent authorities in the Arab countries. The people with whom we have tried, and shall again try, to open a dialogue do not want publicity. In this sensitive field, a hint of publication can be enough to extinguish a spark of hope. Imagination and a broad outlook are required, but imagination must not be allowed to become blindness. Patience and close attention are needed if seeds that have yet to germinate are to yield fruit in the course of time and not be sterilized by the glare of publicity.

At all events, the Government of Israel will neglect no opportunity to develop and foster soundings and contacts that may be of value in blazing a trail, always with scrupulous regard for the secrecy of the contacts, if our interlocutors so prefer.

But what have been the reactions of Arab leaders, so far, to our public proposals for peace? Here are some outstanding examples:

On 26 July 1967, Hussein declared: "The battle which began on 5 June is only one battle in what will become a long war."

On 1 November 1967, the Prime Minister of Israel, the late Levi Eshkol, enumerated five principles of peace, and Nasser's reply on 23 November was: "The Arabs hold steadfastly to the Khartoum decision—no peace, no recognition, and no negotiation with Israel."

From November 1967 until July 1968, Israel sent forth its calls for peace again and again, and on 16 July, the Egyptian Foreign Minister replied:

With regard to Arab policy, I have always reiterated what was agreed upon at Khartoum, that we are not prepared to recognize Israel, to negotiate with it, or to sign a peace with it.

On 8 November 1968, Foreign Minister Abba Eban presented to the General Assembly of the United Nations a detailed peace program in nine clauses:

The establishment of a just and lasting peace;
The determination of secure and recognized borders;
Security agreements, including non-aggression pacts;
Borders open to travel and trade;
Freedom of navigation in international waterways;

63

A solution to the refugee problem through a conference of representatives of the countries of the Middle East, the countries contributing to refugee upkeep, and the United Nations Specialized Agencies to draw up a five-year plan; the conference could be convened even before general peace negotiations began;

The Holy Places of Christianity and Islam in Jerusalem to be placed under the responsibility of the respective faiths, with the aim of formulating agreements which will give force to their universal character;

Mutual recognition of sovereignty;
Regional cooperation in development projects for the good of the whole region.

The Arab leaders disregarded the program and did not even favor it with reply or comment.

On 17 March 1969, the day on which I assumed my present office, I re-emphasized the principles of peace, saying:

We are prepared to discuss peace with our neighbors any day and on all matters. Nasser's reply, three days later, was:

There is no voice transcending the sounds of war, and there must not be such a voice—nor is there any call holier than the call to war.

In the Knesset on 5 May 1969, on 8 May, and on 30 June, I re-enunciated our readiness to enter immediately into negotiations, without prior conditions, with every one of our neighbors, to reach a peace settlement.

The retort of the Arab States was swift. The commentators of Damascus, Amman, and Cairo stigmatized peace as "surrender" and heaped scorn on Israel's proposals. Take, for example, this from Al-Destour, a leading Jordanian newspaper, of 15 June 1969:

"Mrs. Meir is prepared to go to Cairo to hold discussions with President Abdul Nasser, but to her sorrow, has not been invited. She believes that one fine day a world without guns will emerge in the Middle East. Golda Meir is behaving like a grandmother telling bedtime stories to her grandchildren."

And that was the moment for Nasser to announce abrogation of the cease-fire agreements and non-recognition of the cease-fire lines.

On 19 September 1969, the Foreign Minister of Israel appealed in the United Nations to the Arab States to declare their intention to establish a lasting peace, to eliminate the twenty-one-year-old conflict, to hold negotiations for detailed agreement on all the problems with which we are faced.

He referred to Israel's affirmation to Ambassador Jarring on 2 April:

Israel accepts the Security Council Resolution (242) calling for the promotion of agreement for the establishment of a just and lasting peace, reached through negotiation and agreement between the Governments concerned. Implementation of the agreement will commence when accord has been reached on all its provisions.

On 24 September 1969, during my visit to the United States, I was happy to hear that a statement had been made on behalf of the Egyptian Foreign Minister, then in New York, that Egypt was prepared to enter into Rhodes-style peace talks with Israel. I responded forthwith that Israel was willing and, as previously recorded, was prepared to discuss the establishment of a true peace with Egypt at any time and without prior conditions.

Within a few hours, an authoritative dementi came from Cairo. Any Egyptian readiness to enter into Rhodes-style talks was officially denied. The spokesman of the Egyptian Government termed the statement to that effect an "imperialist lie."

On 18 December 1969, the Knesset approved the present Government's basic principles. I quote the following passages:

"The Government will steadfastly strive to achieve a durable peace with Israel's neighbors, founded on peace treaties achieved by direct negotiations between the parties. Agreed, secure and recognized borders will be laid down in the treaties.

The treaties will assure cooperation and mutual aid, the solution of any problem that may be a stumbling-block on the path to peace, and the avoidance of all aggression, direct and indirect. Israel will continue to be willing to negotiate—without prior conditions from either side—with any of the neighboring States for the conclusion of such a treaty.

The Government will be alert for any expression of willingness amongst the Arab nations for peace with Israel and will welcome and respond to any readiness for peace from the Arab States. Israel will persevere in manifesting its peaceful intentions and in explaining the clear advantages to all the peoples of the area of peaceful co-existence, without aggression or subversion, without territorial expansion or intervention in the freedom and internal regimes of the States in the area."

To attain peace, I am ready to go at any hour to any place, to meet any authorized leader of any Arab State—to conduct negotiations with mutual respect, in parity and without pre-conditions, and with a clear recognition that the problems under controversy can be solved. For there is room to fulfill the national aspirations of all the Arab States and of Israel as well in the Middle East, and progress, development, and cooperation can be hastened among all its nations, in place of barren bloodshed and war without end.

If peace does not yet reign, it is from no lack of willingness on our part: it is the inevitable outcome of the refusal of the Arab leadership to make peace with us. That refusal is still a projection of reluctance to be reconciled to the living presence of Israel within secure and recognized boundaries, still a product of the hope, which flickers on in their hearts, that they will accomplish its destruction. And this has been the state of things since 1948, long before the issue of the territories arose in the aftermath of the Six-Day War.

Moreover, if peace does not yet reign, it is equally not because of any lack of "flexibility" on our part, or because of the so-called "rigidity" of our position.

That position is: cease-fire, agreement, and peace. The Arab Governments preach and practice no cease-fire, no negotiation, no agreement, and no peace. Which of the two attitudes is stubborn and unyielding? The Arab Governments' or ours?

It is also argued that, by creating facts on the ground, we are laying down irrevocable conditions, which render negotiations superfluous or make it more difficult to enter into them. This contention, too, is wholly mistaken and unfounded. The refusal of the Arab States to enter into negotiations with us is simply an extension of their long-drawn-out intransigence. It goes back to before the Six-Day War, before there were any settlements in the administered territories.

After that fighting, we said—and we left no room for doubt—that we were willing to enter into negotiations with our neighbors with no pre-conditions on either side. This willingness does not signify that we have no opinions, thoughts, or demands, or that we shall not exercise our right to articulate them in the discussions, as our neighbors are entitled to no less.

Nasser and Hussein, for example, in their official replies to Dr. Jarring, said that they saw the partition borders of 1947 as constituting definitive frontiers. I do not have to explain our attitude to that answer, but we do not insist that, in negotiating with us, the Arab States forfeit their equal right to make any proposal that they think fit, just as they cannot annul from the outset our right to express, in the discussions, any ideas or proposals which we may form. And there assuredly is no moral or political ground for demanding that we refrain from any constructive act in the territories, even though the Arab Governments reject the call for peace and make ready for war.

There is yet another argument touching on our insistence on direct negotiations: it is as devoid as are the others of any least foundation in the annals of international relations or of those between our neighbors and ourselves. For we did sit down face-to-face with the representatives of the Arab States at the time of the negotiations in Rhodes, and no one dare profess that Arab honor was thereby affronted.

There is no precedent of a conflict between nations being brought to finality without direct negotiations. In the conflict between the Arabs and Israel, the issue of direct negotiations goes to the very crux of the matter. For the objective is to achieve peace and co-existence, and how will our neighbors ever be able to live with us in peace if they refuse to speak with us at all?

From the start of the conversations with Ambassador Jarring, we agreed that the face-to-face discussions should take place under the auspices of the Secretary-General's envoy. During 1968, Dr. Jarring sought to bring the parties together under his chairmanship in a neutral place. In March 1968, he proposed that we meet Egypt and Jordan in Nicosia. We agreed, but the Arabs did not.

In the same year, and again in September 1969, we expressed our consent to his proposal that the meetings be held in the manner of the Rhodes talks, which comprised both face-to-face and indirect talks; a number of times it seemed that the Arabs and the Soviets would also fall in with that proposal, but in the end they went back on it.

Only those who deny the right of another State to exist, or who want to avoid recognizing the fact of its sovereignty, can develop the refusal to talk to it into an inculcated philosophy of life which the pupil swears

70

to adhere to as to a political, national principle. The refusal to talk to us directly is damning evidence that the unwillingness of the Arab leaders to be reconciled with the very being of Israel is the basic reason why peace is still to seek.

I am convinced that it is unreal and utopian to think that using the word "withdrawal" will pave the way to peace. True, those among us who do believe that the magic of that word is likely to bring us nearer to peace only mean withdrawal after peace is achieved and then, only to secure and agreed boundaries demarcated in a peace treaty.

On the other hand, when Arab and Soviet leaders talk of "withdrawal," they mean complete and outright retreat from all the administered territories and from Jerusalem, without the making of a genuine peace and without any agreement on new permanent borders, but with an addendum calling for Israel's consent to the return of all the refugees.

Israel's policy is clear, and we shall continue to clarify it at every suitable opportunity, as we have done in the United Nations and elsewhere. No person dedicated to truth could misinterpret our policy: when we speak of secure and recognized boundaries, we do not mean that, after peace is made, the Israel Defense Forces should be deployed beyond the boundaries.

Abraham Lincoln

Gettysburg Address
November 19, 1863

Four score and seven years ago, our fathers brought forth upon this continent a new nation: conceived in liberty and dedicated to the proposition that all men are created equal.

Now, we are engaged in a great civil war—testing whether that nation or any nation so conceived and so dedicated can long endure. We are met on a great battlefield of that war.

We have come to dedicate a portion of that field as a final resting place for those who here gave their lives that that nation might live. It is altogether fitting and proper that we should do this.

But, in a larger sense, we cannot dedicate, we cannot consecrate, we cannot hallow this ground. The brave men, living and dead, who struggled here have consecrated it, far above our poor power to add or detract. The world will little note, nor long remember, what we say here, but it can never forget what they did here.

It is for us the living, rather, to be dedicated here to the unfinished work, which they who fought here have thus far so nobly advanced. It is rather, for us to be here dedicated to the great task remaining before us, that from these honored dead, we take increased devotion to that cause for which they gave the last full measure of devotion; that we here, highly resolve that these dead shall not have died in vain; that this nation, under God, shall have a new birth of freedom., and that government of the people, by the people, for the people, shall not perish from the earth.

Abraham Lincoln

Second Inaugural Address
March 4, 1865

Fellow Countrymen:

At this second appearing, to take the oath of the presidential office, there is less occasion for an extended address than there was at the first. Then a statement, somewhat in detail, of a course to be pursued, seemed fitting and proper. Now, at the expiration of four years, during which public declarations have been constantly called forth on every point and phase of the great contest which still absorbs the attention and engrosses the energies of the nation, little that is new could be presented.

The progress of our arms, upon which all else chiefly depends, is as well known to the public as to myself; and it is, I trust, reasonably satisfactory and encouraging to all. With high hope for the future, no prediction in regard to it is ventured.

On the occasion corresponding to this four years ago, all thoughts were anxiously directed to an impending civil-war. All dreaded it; all sought to avert it. While the inaugural address was being delivered from this place, devoted altogether to saving the Union without war, insurgent agents were in the city seeking to destroy it without war; seeking to dissolve the Union, and divide effects, by negotiation. Both parties deprecated war; but one of them would make war rather than let the nation survive; and the other would accept war rather than let it perish. And the war came.

One eighth of the whole population were colored slaves, not distributed generally over the Union, but localized in the Southern part of it. These slaves constituted a peculiar and powerful interest. All knew that this interest was, somehow, the cause of the war.

To strengthen, perpetuate, and extend this interest was the object for which the insurgents would rend the Union, even by war; while the Government claimed no right to do more than to restrict the territorial enlargement of it. Neither party expected for the war, the magnitude or the duration which it has already attained.

Neither anticipated that the cause of the conflict might cease with, or even before, the conflict itself should cease. Each looked for an easier triumph, and a result less fundamental and astounding. Both read the same Bible and pray to the same God; and each invokes His aid against the other. It may seem strange that any men should dare to ask a just God's assistance in wringing their bread from the sweat of other men's faces; but let us judge not that we be not judged.

The prayers of both could not be answered; that of neither has been answered fully. The Almighty has His own purposes. "Woe unto the world because of offenses! For it must needs be that offenses come; but woe to that man by whom the offense cometh!"

If we shall suppose that American Slavery is one of those offenses which, in the providence of God, must needs come, but which, having continued through His appointed time, He now wills to remove, and that He gives to both North and South this terrible war, as the woe due to those by whom the offense came, shall we discern therein any departure from those divine attributes which the believers in a Living God always ascribe to Him?

Fondly do we hope—fervently do we pray—that this mighty scourge of war may speedily pass away. Yet, if God wills that it continue, until all the wealth piled by the bond-man's two hundred and fifty years of unrequited toil shall be sunk, and until every drop of blood drawn with the lash shall be paid by another drawn with the sword—as was said three thousand years ago, so still it must be said, "the judgments of the Lord are true and righteous altogether."

With malice toward none; with charity for all; with firmness in the right, as God gives us to see the right, let us strive on to finish the work we are in; to bind up the nation's wounds; to care for him who shall have borne the battle, and for his widow, and his orphan— to do all which may achieve and cherish a just and a lasting peace among ourselves and with all nations.

Robert La Follette

Free Speech during Wartime
October 6, 1917

Mr. President: I rise to a question of personal privilege.

I have no intention of taking the time of the Senate with a review of the events which led to our entrance into the war except in so far as they bear upon the question of personal privilege to which I am addressing myself.

Six Members of the Senate and fifty Members of the House voted against the declaration of war. Immediately, there was let loose upon those Senators and Representatives a flood of invective and abuse from newspapers and individuals who had been clamoring for war, unequalled, I believe, in the history of civilized society.

Prior to the declaration of war, every man who had ventured to oppose our entrance into it had been condemned as a coward or worse, and even the President had by no means been immune from these attacks.

Since the declaration of war, the triumphant war press has pursued those Senators and Representative who voted against war with malicious falsehood and recklessly libelous attacks, going to the extreme limit of charging them with treason against their country.

This campaign of libel and character assassination directed against the Members of Congress who opposed our entrance into the war has been continued down to the present hour, and I have upon my desk newspaper clippings, some of them libels upon me alone, some directed as well against other Senators who voted in opposition to the declaration of war.

One of these newspaper reports most widely circulated represents a Federal judge in the State of Texas as saying, in a charge of a grand jury—I read the article as it appeared in the newspaper and the headline with which it is introduced:

District Judge Would Like to Take Shot at Traditions in Congress

Houston, Texas, October 1, 1917. Judge Waller T. Burns, of the United States district court, in charging a Federal grand jury at the beginning of the October term today, after calling by name Senators Stone of Missouri, Hardwick of Georgia, Vardaman of Mississippi, Gronna of North Dakota, Gore of Oklahoma, and LaFollette of Wisconsin, said:

"If I had a wish, I would wish that you men had jurisdiction to return bills of indictment against these men. They ought to be tried promptly and fairly, and I believe this court could administer the law fairly; but I

78

have a conviction, as strong as life, that this country should stand them up against an adobe wall tomorrow and give them what they deserve. If any man deserves death, it is a traitor. I wish that I could pay for the ammunition. I would like to attend the execution, and if I were in the firing squad, I would not want to be the marksman who had the blank shell."

If this newspaper clipping were a single or exceptional instance of lawless defamation, I should not trouble the Senate with a reference to it. But, Mr. President, it is not.

In this mass of newspaper clippings which I have here upon my desk, and which I shall not trouble the Senate to read unless it is desired, and which represent but a small part of the accumulation clipped from the daily press of the country in the last three months, I find other Senators, as well as myself, accused of the highest crimes of which any man can be guilty— treason and disloyalty—and, sir, accused not only with no evidence to support the accusation, but without the suggestion that such evidence anywhere exists.

It is not claimed that Senators who opposed the declaration of war have since that time acted with any concerted purpose, either regarding war measures or any others. They have voted according to their individual opinions, have often been opposed to each other on bills which have come before the Senate since the declaration of war, and, according to my recollection, have never all voted together since that time upon any singe proposition upon which the Senate has been divided.

I am aware, Mr. President, that in pursuance of this campaign of vilification and attempted intimidation, requests from various individuals and certain organizations have been submitted to the Senate for my expulsion from this body, and that such requests have been referred to and considered by one of the committees of the Senate.

If I alone had been made the victim of these attacks, I should not take one moment of the Senate's time for their consideration, and I believe that other Senators who have been unjustly and unfairly assailed, as I have been, hold the same attitude upon this that I do. Neither the clamor of the mob nor the voice of power will ever turn me by the breadth of a hair from the course I mark out for myself, guided by such knowledge as I can obtain and controlled and directed by a solemn conviction of right and duty.

But, sir, it is not alone Members of Congress that the war party in this country has sought to intimidate. The mandate seems to have gone forth to the sovereign people of this country that they must be silent while those things are being done by their Government which most vitally concern their well-being, their happiness, and their lives. Today, and for weeks past, honest and law-abiding citizens of this country are being terrorized and outraged in their rights by those sworn to uphold the laws and protect the rights of the people.

I have in my possession numerous affidavits establishing the fact that people are being unlawfully arrested, thrown into jail, held incommunicado for days, only to be eventually discharged without ever having been taken into court, because they have committed no crime. Private residences are being invaded, loyal citizens of undoubted integrity and probity arrested, cross-examined, and the most sacred constitutional rights guaranteed to every American citizen are being violated.

It appears to be the purpose of those conducting this campaign to throw the country into a state of terror, to coerce public opinion, to stifle criticism, and suppress discussion of the great issues involved in this war.

I think all men recognize that in time of war, the citizen must surrender some rights for the common good which he is entitled to enjoy in time of peace. But, sir, the right to control their own Government according to constitutional forms is not one of the rights that the citizens of this country are called upon to surrender in time of war.

Rather, in time of war, the citizen must be more alert to the preservation of his right to control his Government. He must be most watchful of the encroachment of the military upon the civil power. He must beware of those precedents in support of arbitrary action by administration officials which, excused on the pleas of necessity in war time, become the fixed rule when the necessity has passed and normal conditions have been restored.

More than all, the citizen and his representative in Congress in time of war must maintain his right of free speech.

More than in times of peace, it is necessary that the channels for free public discussion of governmental policies shall be open and unclogged. I believe, Mr. President, that I am now touching upon the most important question in this country today—and that is the right of the citizens of this country and their representatives in Congress to discuss in an orderly way, frankly and publicly and without fear, from the platform and through the press, every important phase of this war, its causes and manner in which it should be conducted, and the terms upon which peace should be made.

The belief, which is becoming widespread in this land, that this most fundamental right is being denied to the citizens of this country is a fact. The tremendous significance of which those in authority have not yet begun to appreciate. I am contending, Mr. President, for the great fundamental right of the sovereign people of this country to make their voice heard and have that voice heeded upon the great questions arising out of this war, including not only how the war shall be prosecuted, but the conditions upon which it may be terminated with a due regard for the rights and the honor of this Nation and the interests of humanity.

I am contending for this right because the exercise of it is necessary to the welfare, to the existence of this Government, to the successful conduct of this war, and to a peace which shall be enduring and for the best interests of this country.

Suppose success attends the attempt to stifle all discussion of the issues of this war, all discussions of the terms upon which it should be concluded, all discussion of the objects and purposes to be accomplished by it, and concede the demand of the war-mad press and war extremists that they monopolize the right of public utterance upon these questions unchallenged. What think you would be the consequences to this country not only during the war but after the war?

Mr. President, our Government, above all others, is founded on the right of the people freely to discuss all matters pertaining to their Government, in war not less than in peace. It is true, sir, that Members of the House of Representatives are elected for two years, the President for four years, and the Members of the Senate for six years, and during their temporary official terms these officers constitute what is called the Government.

But back of them always is the controlling, sovereign power of the People, and when the people can make their will known, the faithful officer will obey that will. Though the right of the People to express their will by ballot is suspended during the term office of the elected official, nevertheless the duty of the official to obey the popular will shall continue throughout his entire term of office. How can that popular will express itself between elections except by meetings, by speeches, by publications, by petitions, and by addresses to the representatives of the people?

Any man who seeks to set a limit upon those rights, whether in war or peace, aims a blow at the most vital part of our Government. And then, as the time for election approaches and the official is called to account for his stewardship—not a day, not a wee, not a month before the election, but a year or more before it, if the people choose—they must have the right to the freest possible discussion of every question upon which their representative has acted, of the merits of every measure he has supported or opposed, of every vote he has cast, and every speech that he has made.

And before this great fundamental right every other must, if necessary, give way. For in no other manner can representative government be preserved.

Adolf Hitler

Declaration of War on the US
Dec 11, 1941

If the Providence has so willed that the German people cannot be spared this fight, then I can only be grateful that it entrusted me with the leadership in this historic struggle which, for the next 500 or 1,000 years, will be described as decisive, not only for the history of Germany, but for the whole of Europe and indeed the whole world.

The German people and their soldiers are working and fighting today, not only for the present, but also for the coming, nay the most distant generations. The Creator has imposed a historical revision on a unique scale upon us.

So far as Germany's attitude toward America is concerned, I have to state:

One: Germany is perhaps the only great nation which has never had a colony either in North or South America, or otherwise displayed there was any political activity, unless mention is made of the emigration of many millions of Germans and of their work, which, however, has only been to the benefit of the American Continent and of the U.S.A.

Two: In the whole history of the coming into being and of the existence of the U.S.A., the German Reich has never adopted a politically unfriendly, let alone a hostile attitude, but on the contrary, with the blood of many of its sons, it helped to defend the U.S.A.

The German Reich never took part in any war against the U.S.A. It itself had war imposed on it by the U.S.A. in 1917, and then for reasons which have been thoroughly revealed by an investigation committee set up by President Roosevelt himself. There are no other differences between the Germans and the American people, either territorial or political, which could possibly touch the interests, let alone the existence of the U.S.A.

There was always a difference of Constitution, but that can't be a reason for hostilities so long as the one state does not try to interfere with the other. America is a Republic, a Democracy, and today is a Republic under strong authoritative leadership. The ocean lies between the two states. The divergences between Capitalist America and Bolshevik Russia, if such conceptions had any truth in them, would be much greater than between America led by a President and Germany led by a Fuhrer.

But it is a fact that the two conflicts between Germany and the U.S.A. were inspired by the same force and caused by two men in the U.S.A: Wilson and Roosevelt.

History has already passed its verdict on Wilson, his name stands for one of the basest breaches of the given word, that led to the disruption not only among the so-called vanquished, but among the victors. This breach of his word alone made possible the dictate of Versailles. We know today that a group of interested financiers stood behind Wilson and made use of this paralytic professor because they hoped for increased business. The German people have had to pay for having believed this man with the collapse of their political and economic existence.

But why is there now another President of the U.S.A. who regards it as his only task to intensify anti-German feeling to the pitch of war? National Socialism came to power in Germany in the same years as Roosevelt was elected President. I understand only too well that a worldwide distance separates Roosevelt's ideas and my ideas.

Roosevelt comes from a rich family and belongs to the class whose path is smoothed in the Democracy. I am the only child of a small, poor family and had to fight my way by work and industry.

When the Great War came, Roosevelt occupied a position where he got to know only its pleasant consequences enjoyed by those who do business while others bleed. I was only one of those who carry out orders, as an ordinary soldier, and naturally returned from the war just as poor as I was in autumn of 1914. I shared the fate of millions, and Franklin Roosevelt only the fate of the so-called upper ten thousand.

After the war, Roosevelt tried his hand at financial speculation; he made profits out of the inflation, out of the misery of others, while I, together with many hundreds of thousands more, lay in hospitals. When Roosevelt finally stepped on the political stage with all the advantages of his class, I was unknown and fought for the resurrection of my people.

When Roosevelt took his place at the head of the U.S.A., he was the candidate of a Capitalistic party which made use of him; when I became Chancellor of the German Reich, I was Fuehrer of the popular movement I had created. The powers behind Roosevelt were those powers I had fought at home. The Brains Trust were composed of people we had fought against in Germany as parasites and removed from public life.

Yet there is something in common between us. Roosevelt took over a State in a very poor economic condition, and I took over a Reich faced with complete ruin, also thanks to Democracy. In the U.S.A. there were 13 million unemployed, and in Germany 7,000,000 part-time workers. The finances of both States were in a bad way, and ordinary economic life could hardly be maintained. A development then started in the U.S.A. and in the German Reich, which will make it easy for posterity to pass a verdict on the correctness of the theories.

88

While an unprecedented revival of economic life, culture and art took place in Germany under National Socialistic leadership within the space of a few years; President Roosevelt did not succeed in bringing about even the slightest improvements in his own country. And yet this work must have been much easier in the U.S.A. where there lived scarcely fifteen people on a square kilometer, as against 140 in Germany.

If such a country does not succeed in assuring economic prosperity, this must be a result either of the bad faith of its leaders in power, or of a total inefficiency on the part of the leading men. In scarcely five years, economic problems had been solved in Germany and unemployment had been overcome. During the same period, President Roosevelt had increased the State Debt of his country to an enormous extent. The decreased value of the dollar had brought about a further disintegration of economic life, without diminishing the unemployment figures.

All this is not surprising if one bears in mind that the men he had called to support him, or rather, the men who had called him, belonged to the Jewish element, whose interests are all for disintegration and never for order. While speculation was being fought in National Socialist Germany, it thrived astoundingly under the Roosevelt regime.

Roosevelt's New Deal legislation was all-wrong. It was actually the biggest failure ever experienced by one man. There can be no doubt that a continuation of this economic policy would have undone this President in peace time, in spite of all his dialectical skill.

This fact was realized and fully appreciated also by many Americans including some of high standing. A threatening opposition was gathering over the head of this man. He guessed that the only salvation for him lay in diverting public attention from home to foreign policy. It is interesting to study in this connection the reports of the Polish Envoy in Washington, Potocki. He repeatedly points out that Roosevelt was fully aware of the danger threatening the card castle of his economic system with collapse, and that he was therefore urgently in need of a diversion in foreign policy.

He was strengthened in this resolve by the Jews surrounding him. Their Old Testament thirst for revenge saw in the U.S.A. an instrument for preparing a second "Purim" for the European nations, which were becoming increasingly anti-Semitic. The full diabolical meanness of Jewry rallied round this man, and he stretched out his hands.

Thus began the increasing efforts of the American President to create conflicts, to do everything to prevent conflicts from being peacefully solved. For years this man harbored one desire: that a conflict should break out somewhere in the world. The most convenient place would be in Europe, where American economy could be committed to the cause of one of the belligerents in such a way that a political interconnection of interests would arise calculated slowly to bring America nearer such a conflict.

This would thereby divert public interest from bankrupt economic policy at home towards foreign problems.

His attitude to the German Reich in this spirit was particularly sharp. In 1937, Roosevelt made a number of speeches, including a particularly mean one pronounced in Chicago on 5th October 1937. Systematically he began to incite American public opinions against Germany. He threatened to establish a kind of Quarantine against the so-called Authoritarian States.

But Mr. Roosevelt went even farther. In contradiction to all the tenets of international law, he declared that he would not recognize certain Governments which did not suit him, would not accept readjustments, would maintain Legations of States dissolved long before or actually set them up as legal Governments. He even went so far as to conclude agreements with such Envoys and thus to acquire a right simply to occupy foreign territories.

I will pass over the insulting attacks made by this so-called President against me. That he calls me a gangster is uninteresting. After all, this expression was not coined in Europe but in America, no doubt because such gangsters are lacking here. Apart from this, I cannot be insulted by Roosevelt for I consider him mad, just as Wilson was.

I don't need to mention what this man has done for years in the same way against Japan. First he incites war, then falsifies the causes, then odiously wraps himself in a cloak of Christian hypocrisy and slowly but surely leads mankind to war, not without calling God to witness the honesty of his attack—in the approved manner of an old Freemason.

As a consequence of the further extension of President Roosevelt's policy, which is aimed at unrestricted world domination and dictatorship, the U.S.A. together with England have not hesitated from using any means to dispute the rights of the German, Italian, and Japanese nations to the base of their natural existence.

The Governments of the U.S.A. and of England have therefore resisted, not only now but also for all time, every just understanding meant to bring about a better New Order in the world. Since the beginning of the war the American president, Roosevelt, has been guilty of a series of the worst crimes against international law; illegal seizure of ships and other property of German and Italian nationals, coupled with the threat to, and looting of, those who were deprived of their liberty by internment.

The Three Powers have therefore concluded the following Agreement, which was signed in Berlin today: "In their unshakable determination not to lay down arms until the joint war against the U.S.A. and England reaches a successful conclusion, the German, Italian, and Japanese governments have agreed on the following points:

Article 1. Germany, Italy, and Japan will wage the common war forced upon them by the U.S.A. and England with all the means of power at their disposal, to a victorious conclusion.

Article II. Germany, Italy, and Japan undertake not to conclude an armistice or peace with the U.S.A., or with England without complete mutual understanding.

Article III. Germany, Italy, and Japan will continue the closest cooperation even after the victorious conclusion of the war in order to bring about a just new order in the sense of the Tri-Partite Pact concluded by them on the 27th September 1940...

Deputies, Members of the German Reichstag:

Ever since my last peace proposal of July 1940 was rejected, we have realized that this struggle has to be fought out to its last implications. That the Anglo-Saxon-Jewish-Capitalist World finds itself now in one and the same Front with Bolshevism does not surprise us National Socialists: we have always found them in company.

Today I am at the head of the strongest Army in the world, the largest Air Force and of a proud Navy. Behind and around me stands the Party with which I became great and which has become great through me. The enemies I see before me are the same enemies as 20 years ago, but the path along which I look forward cannot be compared with that on which I look back...

The American President and his Plutocratic clique have mocked us as the Have-nots—that is true, but the Have-nots will see to it that they are not robbed of the little they have.

You, my fellow party members, know my unalterable determination to carry a fight once begun to its successful conclusion. You know my determination in such a struggle to be deterred by nothing, to break every resistance, which must be broken. In September 1939, I assured you that neither force of arms nor time would overcome Germany. I will assure my enemies that neither force of arms, nor time, nor any internal doubts can make us waver in the performance of our duty.

Joseph Stalin

Anniversary of the October Revolution
November 7, 1941

Comrades, Red Army and Red Navy men, commanders and political instructors, men and women workers, men and women collective farmers, intellectuals, brothers and sisters in the enemy rear, who have temporarily fallen under the yoke of the German brigands, our glorious men and women guerrillas who are disrupting the rear of the German invaders!

On behalf of the Soviet Government and our Bolshevik Party, I greet you and congratulate you on the 24th anniversary of the great October Socialist Revolution.

Comrades, today we must celebrate the 24th anniversary of the October Revolution in difficult conditions. The German brigands' treacherous attack and the war that they forced upon us have created a threat to our country. We have temporarily lost a number of regions, and the enemy is before the gates of Leningrad and Moscow.

The enemy calculated that our army would be dispersed at the very first blow and our country forced to its knees. But the enemy wholly miscalculated. Despite temporary reverses, our army and our navy are bravely beating off enemy attacks along the whole front, inflicting heavy losses, while our country—our whole country—has organized itself into a single fighting camp in order, jointly with our army and navy, to rout the German invaders.

There was a time when our country was in a still more difficult position. Recall the year 1918, when we celebrated the first anniversary of the October Revolution. At that time, three-quarters of our country was in the hands of foreign interventionists. We had temporarily lost the Ukraine, the Caucasus, Central Asia, the Urals, Siberia, and the Far East. We had no allies; we had no Red Army; we had only just begun to create it—and we experienced a shortage of bread, a shortage of arms, a shortage of equipment.

At that time, 14 states were arrayed against our country, but we did not become despondent or downhearted. In the midst of the conflagration of war, we organized the Red Army and converted our country into a military camp. The spirit of the great Lenin inspired us at that time for the war against the interventionists.

And what happened? We defeated the interventionists, regained all our lost territories, and achieved victory.

Today, our country is in a far better position than it was 23 years ago. Today, it is many times richer in industry, food, and raw materials. Today, we have allies who jointly with us form a united front against the German invaders. Today, we enjoy the sympathy and support of all the peoples of Europe fallen under the yoke of Fascist tyranny. Today, we have a splendid army and a splendid navy, defending the freedom and independence of our country with their lives. We experience no serious shortage either of food or of arms or equipment.

Our whole country, all the peoples of our country, are backing our army and our navy, helping them smash the Nazi hordes. Our reserves in manpower are inexhaustible. The spirit of the great Lenin inspires us for our patriotic war, today, as it did 23 years ago.

Is it possible, then, to doubt that we can and must gain victory over the German invaders? The enemy is not as strong as some terror-stricken pseudo-intellectuals picture him. The devil is not as terrible as he is painted. Who can deny that our Red Army has more than once put the much-vaunted German troops to panicky flight?

If one judges by Germany's real position and not by the boastful assertions of German propagandists, it will not be difficult to see that the Nazi German invaders are facing disaster.

Hunger and poverty reign in Germany. In four and a half months of war, Germany has lost four and a half million soldiers. Germany is bleeding white; her manpower is giving out. A spirit of revolt is gaining possession, not only of the nations of Europe under the German invaders' yoke, but of the Germans themselves, who see no end to the war.

The German invaders are straining their last forces. There is no doubt that Germany cannot keep up such an effort for any long time. Another few months, another half year, one year perhaps—and Hitlerite Germany must collapse under the weight of its own crimes.

Comrades, Red Army and Red Navy men, commanders and political instructors, men and women guerrillas!

The whole world is looking to you as a force capable of destroying the brigand hordes of German invaders. The enslaved peoples of Europe under the yoke of the German invaders are looking to you as their liberators. A great mission of liberation has fallen to your lot.

Be worthy of this mission! The war you are waging is a war of liberation, a just war. Let the heroic images of our great ancestors—Alexander Nevsky, Dmitri Donskoi, Kusma Minin, Dmitri Pozharsky, Alexander Suvorov, Mikhail Kutuzov—inspire you in this war!

Let the victorious banner of the great Lenin fly over your heads!

Utter destruction to the German invaders!

Death to the German armies of occupation!

98

Long live our glorious motherland, her freedom, and her independence!

Under the banner of Lenin—onward to victory!

Benito Mussolini

To the Blackshirts of Rome
February 23, 1941

Blackshirts of Rome! I come among you to look you firmly in the eyes, feel your temperature and break the silence which is dear to-me, especially in wartime. Have you ever asked yourselves, in an hour of meditation, which every one finds during the day, how long we have been at war? Not only eight months, as a superficial observer of events might believe, not from Sept. 1, 1939, when through guarantees to Poland, Britain unleashed the conflagration with a criminal and premeditated will.

We have been at war six years, precisely from Feb. 1, 1935, when the first communiqué announcing the mobilization of Peloritana was issued.

The Ethiopian war was hardly finished when, from the other shore of the Mediterranean, there reached us appeals from General Franco, who had begun his national revolution. Could we Fascisti leave without answer that cry and remain indifferent in the face of the perpetuation of the bloody crimes of the so-called popular fronts?

Could we refuse to give our aid to the movement of salvation that had found in Antonio Primo de Rivera its creator, ascetic, and martyr? No. Thus, our first squadron of airplanes left on July 27, 1936, and during the same day, we had our first dead.

We have actually been at war since 1922—that is from the day when we lifted the flag of our revolution, which was then defended by a handful of men against the Masonic, democratic, capitalistic world. From that day—world liberalism, democracy, and plutocracy declared and waged war against us with press campaigns—spreading libelous reports, financial sabotage, attempts and plots, even when we were intent upon the work of international reconstruction, which is and will remain for centuries, as the undestroyable documentation of our creative will.

With the outbreak of hostilities on Sept. 1, 1939, we had just finished two wars, which imposed relatively modest sacrifices in human life but had forced us to make an enormous logistic and financial effort.

The lightning-like and crushing victory of Germany in the West eliminated the eventuality of a long continental war. Since then, the land war on the Continent has ended and it cannot flare back. The German victory was facilitated by Italian non-belligerency, which immobilized heavy naval, air, and land forces of the Anglo-French bloc. Some people, who today apparently think Italy's intervention was premature, were probably the same who then I deemed it too late.

In reality, the moment was timely because if it is true that one enemy was in the course of liquidation, there remained the other—the bigger one, the most powerful enemy number one against whom we are engaged and against whom we will continue the struggle to the last drop of blood.

Having definitely liquidated Britain's armies on the European Continent, the war could not but assume a naval, air, and for us, also a colonial character. It is the geographic and historic order of things that the most difficult and most faraway theatres of war are reserved for Italy: War beyond the sea and in the desert.

Our fronts stretch for thousands of kilometers and are thousands of kilometers away. Some ignorant foreign commentators should take due account of this. However, during the first four months of the war, we were able to inflict grave naval, air, and land blows to the forces of the British Empire.

Since 1935, the attention of our general staff has been focused on Libya. All the work of the Governors, who succeeded each other in Libya, was aimed at strengthening economically and militarily that large region, transforming the former desert or desert zones into fecund land. Miracles!

This word is able to sum up what has been done down there. With European tension becoming graver, and following the events of 1935 and 1936—Libya, re-conquered by Fascism, was considered one of the most delicate points in our general strategic setup, since it could be attacked from two fronts.

The effort carried out militarily to strengthen Libya is shown by these figures.

Only during the period that goes from Oct. 1, 1937, to Jan. 31, 1940—were sent to Libya, 14,000 officers and 396,358 soldiers, and organized two armies—the fifth and tenth. This latter had ten divisions.

In the same period were sent 1,924 cannon of all calibers and many of them of recent construction and model, 15,386 machine-guns, 11,000,000 rounds of shells, 1,344,287,275 bullets for light arms, 127,877 tons of engineers' materials, 779 tanks with a certain percentage of heavy tanks, 9,584 auto vehicles of various kinds, 4,809 motorcycles.

We are not like the English. We boast that we are not like them. We haven't elevated lying into a government art nor into a narcotic for the people, the way the London government has done. We call bread bread and wine wine, and when the enemy wins a battle, it is useless and ridiculous to seek, as the English do in their incomparable hypocrisy, to deny or diminish it.

One entire army—the Tenth—was broken up almost completely with its men and cannon. The Fifth Air Squadron was literally sacrificed, almost entirely. Where possible, we resisted strongly and furiously.

Since we recognize these facts, it is useless for the enemy to exaggerate the figures of its booty. It is

103

because we are certain, regarding the grade of national maturity reached by the Italian people and regarding the future development of events, that we continue to follow the cult of truth and repudiate all falsification.

The events during these months exasperate our will and must accentuate against the enemy that cold, conscious, implacable hate—hate in every home, which is indispensable for victory.

Neutrals of every continent, who are spectators at the bloody clashes between the armed masses, must have sufficient shame to keep quiet and not express libelous provocative opinions.

The Italian prisoners, who fell into the hands of the Greeks, are a few thousand—most of them wounded. The Greek successes do not go out of the tactical field and only megalomania has magnified them. The Greek losses are very high, and shortly it will be Spring, and as befits such a season our season—beautiful things will grow. I say beautiful things will be seen in every one of the four cardinal points.

Great Britain cannot win the war. I can prove this logically and in this case belief is corroborated by fact. This proof begins with the dogmatic premise that although anything may happen, Italy will march with Germany, side by side, to the end.

Those who may be tempted to imagine something different forget that the alliance between Italy and Germany is not only between two States or two armies or two diplomacies, but between two peoples and two

104

revolutions and is destined to give its imprint upon the century.

The collaboration offered by the Fuehrer and that which the German air and armored units are giving in the Mediterranean are proof that all fronts are common and that our efforts are common. The Germans know that Italy today has on her shoulders the weight of 1,000,000 British and Greek soldiers, of from 1,500 to 2,000 planes, of as many tanks, of thousands of cannon, of at least 500,000 tons of military shipping.

Cooperation between the two armed forces occurs on the plan of comradely, loyal, spontaneous solidarity. Let it be said for foreigners, who are always ready to libel, that the comportment of German soldiers in Sicily and Libya is, under all respects, perfect and worthy of a strong army and a strong people brought up under severe discipline.

Let me say now that what is occurring in the United States is one of the most colossal mystifications in all history. Illusion and lying are the basis of American interventionism—illusion that the United States is still a democracy, when instead it is a political and financial oligarchy dominated by Jews, through a personal form of dictatorship. The lie is that the Axis powers, after they finish Great Britain, want to attack America.

Neither in Rome nor Berlin are such fantastic plans as this prepared. These projects could not be made by those who have an inclination for the madhouse. Though we certainly are totalitarian and will always be so, we have our feet on hard ground. Americans who will read what I say, should be calm and not believe in the existence of a big bad wolf who wants to devour them.

In all cases, it is more likely that the United States, before it is attacked by Axis soldiers, will be attacked by the not well known but very warlike inhabitants of the planet Mars, who will descend from the stratosphere in unimaginable flying fortresses.

Rome comrades! Through you I want to speak to the Italian people, to the authentic, real, great Italian people, who fight with the courage of lions on land, sea, and air fronts; people who early in the morning are up to go to work in fields, factories, and offices; people who do not permit themselves luxuries, not even innocent ones.

They absolutely must not be confused or contaminated by the minority or well-known poltroons, anti-social individuals and complainers, who grumble about rations and regret their suspended comforts, or by snakes, the remains of the Masonic lodges, whom we will crush without difficulties when and how we want.

The Italian people, the Fascist people, deserve and will have victory. The hardships, suffering, and sacrifices that are faced with exemplary courage and dignity by the Italian people will have their day of compensation when all the enemy forces are crushed on the battlefields by the heroism of our soldiers—and a triple, immense cry will cross the mountains and oceans like lightning and light new hopes and give new certainties to spirit multitudes: Victory, Italy, peace with justice among peoples!

Napoleon Bonaparte

Proclamation during the Italian Campaign
April 26, 1796

In a fortnight, you have won six victories, taken twenty-one standards, fifty-five pieces plains in the world. Rich provinces, great of artillery, several strong positions, and conquered the richest part of Piedmont; you have captured 15,000 prisoners and killed or wounded more than 10,000 men.

You have won battles without cannon, crossed rivers without bridges, made forced marches without shoes, camped without brandy and often without bread. Soldiers of liberty, only republican phalanxes could have endured what you have endured. Soldiers, you have our thanks! The grateful Patrie will owe its prosperity to you.

The two armies, which but recently attacked you with audacity, are fleeing before you in terror; the wicked men who laughed at your misery and rejoiced at the thought of the triumphs of your enemies are confounded and trembling.

But, soldiers, as yet you have done nothing compared with what remains to be done.

Undoubtedly the greatest obstacles have been overcome—but you still have battles to fight, cities to

108

capture, rivers to cross. Is there one among you whose courage is abating? No. All of you are consumed with a desire to extend the glory of the French people; all of you long to humiliate those arrogant kings who dare to contemplate placing us in fetters; all of you desire to dictate a glorious peace, one which will indemnify the Patrie for the immense sacrifices it has made; all of you wish to be able to say with pride, as you return to your villages, "I was with the victorious army of Italy!"

Friends, I promise you this conquest; but there is one condition you must swear to fulfill—to respect the people whom you liberate, to repress the horrible pillaging committed by scoundrels incited by our enemies. Otherwise you would not be the liberators of the people; you would be their scourge. Plunderers will be shot without mercy; already, several have been.

Peoples of Italy, the French army comes to break your chains; the French people is the friend of all peoples; approach it with confidence; your property, your religion, and your customs will be respected.

We are waging war as generous enemies, and we wish only to crush the tyrants who enslave you.

Woodrow Wilson

American Declaration of War on Germany
April 2, 1917

Gentlemen of the Congress:

I have called the Congress into extraordinary session because there are serious, very serious, choices of policy to be made, and made immediately, which it was neither right nor constitutionally permissible that I should assume the responsibility of making.

On the third of February last, I officially laid before you the extraordinary announcement of the Imperial German Government that on and after the first day of February it was its purpose to put aside all restraints of law or of humanity, and use its submarines to sink every vessel that sought to approach either the ports of Great Britain and Ireland, or the western coasts of Europe, or any of the ports controlled by the enemies of Germany within the Mediterranean.

That had seemed to be the object of the German submarine warfare earlier in the war, but since April of last year, the Imperial Government had somewhat restrained the commanders of its undersea craft in conformity with its promise then given to us that passenger boats should not be sunk, and that due warning would be given to all other vessels which its submarines might seek to destroy—when no resistance was offered or escape attempted, and care taken that their crews were given at least a fair chance to save their lives in their open boats.

The precautions taken were meager and haphazard enough, as was proved in distressing instance after instance in the progress of the cruel and unmanly business. But a certain degree of restraint was observed.

The new policy has swept every restriction aside. Vessels of every kind, whatever their flag, their character, their cargo, their destination, their errand, have been ruthlessly sent to the bottom without warning and without thought of help or mercy for those on board, the vessels of friendly neutrals along with those of belligerents. Even hospital ships and ships carrying relief to the sorely bereaved and stricken people of Belgium, though the latter were provided with safe conduct through the proscribed areas by the German Government itself and were distinguished by unmistakable marks of identity, haven been sunk with the same reckless lack of compassion or of principle.

I was, for a little while, unable to believe that such things would in fact be done by any government that hitherto subscribed to the humane practices of civilized nations. International law had its origin in the attempt to set up some law which would be respected and observed upon the seas, where no nation had right of dominion and where lay the free highways of the world. By painful stage after stage has that law been built up, with meager enough results, indeed, after all was accomplished that could be accomplished, but always with a clear view, at least, of what the heart and conscience of mankind demanded.

This minimum of right the German Government has swept aside under the plea of retaliation and necessity, and because it had no weapons which it could use at sea, except these which it is impossible to employ as it is employing them, without throwing to the winds all scruples of humanity or of respect for the understandings that were supposed to underlie the intercourse of the world.

I am not now thinking of the loss of property involved, immense and serious as that is, but only of the wanton and wholesale destruction of the lives of non-combatants, men, women, and children engaged in pursuits which have always, even in the darkest periods of modern history, been deemed innocent and legitimate. Property can be paid for; the lives of peaceful and innocent people cannot be.

The present German submarine warfare against commerce is a warfare against mankind.

It is war against all nations.

American ships have been sunk; American lives taken in ways which it has stirred us very deeply to learn of, but the ships and people of other neutral and friendly nations have been sunk and overwhelmed in the waters in the same way. There has been no discrimination. The challenge is to all mankind.

Each nation must decide for itself how it will meet it. The choice we make for ourselves must be made with a moderation of counsel and temperateness of judgment befitting our character and our motives as a nation. We must put excited feeling away. Our motive will not be revenge or the victorious assertion of the physical might of the nation, but only the vindication of right, of human right, of which we are only a single champion.

When I addressed the Congress on the twenty-sixth of February last, I thought that it would suffice to assert our neutral rights with arms, our right to use the seas against unlawful interference, our right to keep our people safe against unlawful violence. But armed neutrality, it now appears, is impracticable. Because submarines are, in effect, outlaws when used as the German submarines have been used against merchant shipping, it is impossible to defend ships against their attacks as the law of nations has assumed that merchantmen would defend themselves against privateers or cruisers, visible craft giving chase upon the open sea. It is common prudence in such circumstances, grim necessity indeed, to endeavor to destroy them before they have shown their own intention. They must be dealt with upon sight, if dealt with at all.

The German Government denies the right of neutrals to use arms at all within the areas of the sea which it has proscribed, even in the defense of rights which no modern publicist has ever before questioned their right to defend. The intimation is conveyed that the armed guards which we have placed on our merchant ships will be treated as beyond the pale of law and subject to be dealt with as pirates would be.

Armed neutrality is ineffectual enough at best; in such circumstances and in the face of such pretensions, it is worse than ineffectual; it is likely only to produce what it was meant to prevent; it is practically certain to draw us into the war without either the rights or the effectiveness of belligerents.

There is one choice we cannot make, we are incapable of making: we will not choose the path of submission and suffer the most sacred rights of our nation and our people to be ignored or violated. The wrongs against which we now array ourselves are no common wrongs: they cut to the very roots of human life.

With a profound sense of the solemn and even tragical character of the step I am taking and of the grave responsibilities which it involves, but in unhesitating obedience to what I deem my constitutional duty, I advise that the Congress declare the recent course of the Imperial German Government to be, in fact, nothing less than war against the government and people of the United States; that it formally accept the status of belligerent, which has thus been thrust upon it; and that it take immediate steps not only to put the country in a more thorough state of defense, but also to exert all its power and employ all its resources to bring the Government of the German Empire to terms and end the war.

What this will involve is clear.

It will involve the utmost practicable cooperation, in counsel and action, with the governments now at war with Germany, and, as incident to that, the extension to those governments of the most liberal financial credits, in order that our resources may so far as possible be added to theirs.

It will involve the organization and mobilization of all the material resources of the country to supply the materials of war and serve the incidental needs of the nation in the most abundant and yet the most economical and efficient way possible.

It will involve the immediate full equipment of the navy in all respects but particularly in supplying it with the best means of dealing with the enemy's submarines.

It will involve the immediate addition to the armed forces of the United States already provided for by law in case of war at least five hundred thousand men, who should, in my opinion, be chosen upon the principle of universal liability to service, and also the authorization of subsequent additional increments of equal force, so soon as they may be needed and can be handled in training.

It will involve also, of course, the granting of adequate credits to the Government, sustained, I hope, so far as they can equitably be sustained by the present generation, by well conceived taxation.

I say sustained so far as may be equitable by taxation because it seems to me that it would be most unwise to base the credits, which will now be necessary entirely on money borrowed. It is our duty, I most respectfully urge, to protect our people so far as we may against the very serious hardships and evils which would be likely to arise out of the inflation which would be produced by vast loans.

In carrying out the measures by which these things are to be accomplished, we should keep constantly in mind, the wisdoms of interfering as little as possible in our own preparation and in the equipment of our own military forces with the duty—for it will be a very practical duty—of supplying the nations already at war with Germany with the materials which they can obtain only from us or by our assistance. They are in the field and we should help them in every way to be effective there.

I shall take the liberty of suggesting, through the several executive departments of the government, for the consideration of your committees, measures for

116

the accomplishment of the several objects I have mentioned. I hope that it will be your pleasure to deal with them as having been framed after very careful thought by the branch of the Government upon which the responsibility of conducting the war, safeguarding the nation will most directly fall.

While we do these things, these deeply momentous things, let us be very clear, and make very clear to all the world what our motives and our objects are. My own thought has not been driven from its habitual and normal course by the unhappy events of the last two months, and I do not believe that the thought of the nation has been altered or clouded by them. I have exactly the same things in mind now that I had in mind when I addressed the Senate on the twenty-second of January last; the same that I had in mind when I addressed the Congress on the third day of February and on the twenty-sixth of February.

Our object now, as then, is to vindicate the principles of peace and justice in the life of the world as against selfish and autocratic power, and to set up amongst the really free and self-governed peoples of the world such a concert of purpose and of action, as will henceforth ensure the observance of those principles.

Neutrality is no longer feasible or desirable where the peace of the world is involved and the freedom of its peoples, and the menace to that peace and freedom lies in the existence of autocratic governments backed by organized force which is controlled wholly by their

117

will, not by the will of their people. We have seen the last of neutrality in such circumstances. We are at the beginning of an age in which it will be insisted that the same standards of conduct and responsibility for wrong done shall be observed among nations and their governments that are observed among the individual citizens of civilized states.

We have no quarrel with the German people. We have no feeling towards them but one of sympathy and friendship. It was not upon their impulse that their government acted in entering this war. It was not with their previous knowledge or approval.

It was a war determined upon as wars used to be determined upon in the old, unhappy days when peoples were nowhere consulted by their rulers, and wars were provoked and waged in the interest of dynasties or of little groups of ambitious men who were accustomed to use their fellow men as pawns and tools.

Self-governed nations do not fill their neighbor states with spies or set the course of intrigue to bring about some critical posture of affairs which will give them an opportunity to strike and make conquest. Such designs can be successfully worked out only under cover and where no one has the right to ask questions. Cunningly contrived plans of deception or aggression, carried, it may be, from generation to generation, can be worked out and kept from the light only within the privacy of courts or behind carefully guarded confidences of a

118

narrow and privileged class. They are happily impossible where public opinion commands and insists upon full information concerning all the nation's affairs.

A steadfast concert for peace can never be maintained except by a partnership of democratic nations. No autocratic government could be trusted to keep faith within it or observe its covenants. It must be a league of honor, a partnership of opinion. Intrigue would eat its vitals away; the plottings of inner circles, who could plan what they would and render account to no one, would be a corruption seated at its very heart.

Only free peoples can hold their purpose and their honor steady to a common end, and prefer the interests of mankind to any narrow interest of their own.

Does not every American feel that assurance has been added to our hope for the future peace of the world by the wonderful and heartening things that have been happening within the last few weeks in Russia? Russia was known, by those who knew it best, to have been always, in fact, democratic at heart—in all the vital habits of her thought, in all the intimate relationships of her people that spoke their natural instinct, their habitual attitude towards life.

The autocracy that crowned the summit of her political structure, long as it had stood and terrible as was the reality of its power, was not in fact Russian in origin,

119

character, or purpose; and now it has been shaken off and the great, generous Russian people have been added in all their naïve majesty and might to the forces that are fighting for freedom in the world, for justice, and for peace. Here is a fit partner for a League of Honor.

One of the things that has served to convince us that the Prussian autocracy was not and could never be our friend, is that from the very outset of the present war, it has filled our unsuspecting communities and even our offices of government with spies, and set criminal intrigues everywhere afoot against our national unity of counsel, our peace within and without, our industries and our commerce.

Indeed, it is now evident that its spies were here even before the war began; and it is unhappily not a matter of conjecture, but a fact proved in our courts of justice that the intrigues which have, more than once, come perilously near to disturbing the peace and dislocating the industries of the country, have been carried on at the instigation, with the support, and even under the personal direction of official agents of the Imperial Government accredited to the Government of the United States.

Even in checking these things and trying to extirpate them, we have sought to put the most generous interpretation possible upon them because we know that their source lay, not in any hostile feeling or purpose of the German people towards us—who were, no doubt, as ignorant of them as we ourselves were—but only in the selfish designs of a Government that did what it pleased and told its people nothing. But they have played their part in serving to convince us at last that that Government entertains no real friendship for us and means to act against our peace and security at its convenience. That it means to stir up enemies against us, at our very doors, that intercepted note to the German Minister at Mexico City is eloquent evidence.

We are accepting this challenge of hostile purpose because we know that in such a government, following such methods, we can never have a friend; and that in the presence of its organized power, always lying in wait to accomplish we know not what purpose, there can be no assured security of the democratic governments of the world. We are now about to accept a gauge of battle with this natural foe to liberty and shall, if necessary, spend the whole force of the nation to check and nullify its pretensions and its power.

We are glad, now that we see the facts with no veil of false pretense about them, to fight thus for the ultimate peace of the world and for the liberation of its peoples—the German peoples included—for the rights of nations great and small, and the privilege of men everywhere, to choose their way of life and of obedience.

The world must be made safe for democracy.

Its peace must be planted upon the tested foundations of political liberty. We have no selfish ends to serve.

We desire no conquest, no dominion. We seek no indemnities for ourselves, no material compensation for the sacrifices we shall cheerfully make. We are but one of the champions of the rights of mankind. We shall be satisfied when those rights have been made as secure as the faith and the freedom of nations can make them.

Just because we fight without rancor and without selfish object, seeking nothing for ourselves, but what we shall wish to share with all free peoples, we shall, I feel confident, conduct our operations as belligerents without passion, and ourselves observe with proud punctilio the principles of right and fair play we profess to be fighting for. I have said nothing of the governments allied with the Imperial Government of Germany because they have not made war upon us or challenged us to defend our right and our honor.

The Austro-Hungarian Government has indeed avowed its unqualified endorsement and acceptance of the reckless and lawless submarine warfare adopted now without disguise by the Imperial German Government. And it has therefore not been possible for this Government to receive Count Tarnowski, the Ambassador recently accredited to this Government by the Imperial and Royal Government of Austria-Hungary; but that Government has not actually engaged in warfare against citizens of the United

122

States on the seas, and I take the liberty, for the present at least, of postponing a discussion of our relations with the authorities at Vienna.

We enter this war only where we are clearly forced into it because there are no other means of defending our rights.

It will be all the easier for us to conduct ourselves as belligerents, in a high spirit of right and fairness, because we act without animus, not in enmity towards a people or with the desire to bring any injury or disadvantage upon them, but only armed opposition to an irresponsible government which has thrown aside all considerations of humanity, and of right, and is running amuck.

We are, let me say again, the sincere friends of the German people, and shall desire nothing so much as the early reestablishment of intimate relations of mutual advantage between us—however hard it may be for them, for the time being, to believe that this is spoken from our hearts.

We have borne with their present government, through all these bitter months, because of that friendship— exercising a patience and forbearance which would otherwise have been impossible.

We shall, happily, still have an opportunity to prove that friendship in our daily attitude and actions towards the millions of men and women of German birth and native, sympathy who live amongst us and share our life, and we shall be proud to prove it towards all who are, in fact, loyal to their neighbors and to the Government in the hour of test.

They are, most of them, as true and loyal Americans as if they had never known any other fealty or allegiance. They will be prompt to stand with us in rebuking and restraining the few who may be of a different mind and purpose. If there should be disloyalty, it will be dealt with a firm hand of stern repression; but, if it lifts its head at all, it will lift it only here and there and without countenance except from a lawless and malignant few.

It is a distressing and oppressive duty, Gentlemen of the Congress, which I have performed in thus addressing you. There are, it may be, many months of fiery trial and sacrifice ahead of us. It is a fearful thing to lead this great peaceful people into war, into the most terrible and disastrous of all wars—civilization itself seeming to be in the balance.

But the right is more precious than peace, and we shall fight for the things which we have always carried nearest our hearts—for democracy, for the right of those who submit to authority to have a voice in their own governments, for the rights and liberties of small nations, for a universal dominion of right by such a concert of free peoples—as shall bring peace and safety to all nations and make the world at last free.

124

To such a task we can dedicate our lives and our fortunes, everything that we are and everything that we have, with the pride of those who know that the day has come when America is privileged to spend her blood and her might for the principles that gave her birth and happiness and the peace which she has treasured. God helping her, she can do no other.

Franklin D. Roosevelt

Pearl Harbor Address
December 8, 1941

Mr. Vice President, Mr. Speaker, Members of the Senate, and of the House of Representatives:

Yesterday, December 7th, 1941—a date which will live in infamy—the United States of America was suddenly and deliberately attacked by naval and air forces of the Empire of Japan.

The United States was at peace with that nation and, at the solicitation of Japan, was still in conversation with its government and its emperor looking toward the maintenance of peace in the Pacific.

Indeed, one hour after Japanese air squadrons had commenced bombing in the American island of Oahu, the Japanese ambassador to the United States and his colleague delivered to our Secretary of State a formal reply to a recent American message. And while this reply stated that it seemed useless to continue the existing diplomatic negotiations, it contained no threat or hint of war or of armed attack.

It will be recorded that the distance of Hawaii from Japan makes it obvious that the attack was deliberately planned many days or even weeks ago. During the intervening time, the Japanese government has

126

deliberately sought to deceive the United States by false statements and expressions of hope for continued peace.

The attack yesterday on the Hawaiian islands has caused severe damage to American naval and military forces. I regret to tell you that very many American lives have been lost. In addition, American ships have been reported torpedoed on the high seas between San Francisco and Honolulu.

Yesterday, the Japanese government also launched an attack against Malaya.

Last night, Japanese forces attacked Hong Kong.

Last night, Japanese forces attacked Guam.

Last night, Japanese forces attacked the Philippine Islands.

Last night, the Japanese attacked Wake Island.

And this morning, the Japanese attacked Midway Island.

Japan has, therefore, undertaken a surprise offensive extending throughout the Pacific area. The facts of yesterday and today speak for themselves. The people of the United States have already formed their opinions and well understand the implications to the very life and safety of our nation.

As commander in chief of the Army and Navy, I have directed that all measures be taken for our defense. But always, will our whole nation remember the character of the onslaught against us.

No matter how long it may take us to overcome this premeditated invasion, the American people in their righteous might will win through to absolute victory.

I believe that I interpret the will of the Congress and of the people when I assert that we will not only defend ourselves to the uttermost, but will make it very certain that this form of treachery shall never again endanger us.

Hostilities exist. There is no blinking at the fact that our people, our territory, and our interests are in grave danger.

With confidence in our armed forces, with the unbounding determination of our people, we will gain the inevitable triumph—so help us God.

I ask that the Congress declare that since the unprovoked and dastardly attack by Japan on Sunday, December 7th, 1941, a state of war has existed between the United States and the Japanese empire.

Franklin D. Roosevelt

Declaration of War on Japan
December 8, 1941

The sudden criminal attacks perpetrated by the Japanese in the Pacific provide the climax of a decade of international immorality.

Powerful and resourceful gangsters have banded together to make war upon the whole human race. Their challenge has now been flung at the United States of America. The Japanese have treacherously violated the long-standing peace between us. Many American soldiers and sailors have been killed by enemy action; American ships have been sunk; American airplanes have been destroyed.

The Congress and the people of the United States have accepted that challenge.

Together with other free peoples, we are now fighting to maintain our right to live among our world neighbors in freedom and in common decency, without fear of assault.

I have prepared the full record of our past relations with Japan, and it will be submitted to the Congress. It begins with the visit of Commodore Perry to Japan eighty-eight years ago. It ends with the visit of two Japanese emissaries to the Secretary of State last

Sunday, an hour after Japanese forces had loosed their bombs and machine guns against our flag, our forces, and our citizens.

I can say with utmost confidence that no Americans today or a thousand years hence need feel anything but pride in our patience and in our efforts through all the years toward achieving a peace in the Pacific, which would be fair and honorable to every nation, large or small. And no honest person, today or a thousand years hence, will be able to suppress a sense of indignation and horror at the treachery committed by the military dictators of Japan under the very shadow of the flag of peace borne by their special envoys in our midst.

The course that Japan has followed for the past ten years in Asia has paralleled the course of Hitler and Mussolini in Europe and in Africa. Today, it has become far more than a parallel. It is collaboration, actual collaboration, so well calculated that all the continents of the world and all the oceans are now considered by the Axis strategists as one gigantic battlefield.

In 1931, ten years ago, Japan invaded Manchukuo—without warning. In 1935, Italy invaded Ethiopia—without warning. In 1938, Hitler occupied Austria—without warning. In 1939, Hitler invaded Czecho-Slovakia—without warning.

Later in 1939, Hitler invaded Poland—without warning. In 1940, Hitler invaded Norway, Denmark, the

Netherlands, Belgium and Luxembourg—without warning. In 1940 Italy attacked France and later Greece—without warning. And in this year 1941, the Axis powers attacked Yugoslavia and Greece and they dominated the Balkans—without warning.

In 1941 also, Hitler invaded Russia—without warning. And now Japan has attacked Malaya and Thailand—and the United States—without warning.

It is all one pattern.

We are now in this war. We are all in it—all the way. Every single man, woman, and child is a partner in the most tremendous undertaking of our American history. We must share together the bad news and the good news, the defeats and the victories—the changing fortunes of war.

So far, the news has been all bad. We have suffered a serious set-back in Hawaii. Our forces in the Philippines, which include the brave people of that commonwealth, are taking punishment, but are defending themselves vigorously. The reports from Guam and Wake and Midway Islands are still confused, but we must be prepared for the announcement that all these outposts have been seized.

The casualty lists of these first few days will undoubtedly be large. I deeply feel the anxiety of all families of the men in our armed forces and the relatives of people in cities which have been bombed. I can only give them my solemn promise that they will get news just as quickly as possible.

This government will put its trusts in the stamina of the American people and will give the facts to the public as soon as two American people fulfilled; first, that the information has been definitely and officially confirmed; and, second, that the release of the information at the time it is received will not prove valuable to the enemy directly or indirectly.

Most earnestly I urge my countrymen to reject all rumors. These ugly little hints of complete disaster fly thick and fast in wartime.

Now a word about the recent past—and the future. A year and a half has elapsed since the fall of France, when the whole world first realized the mechanized might which the Axis nations had been building for so many years. America has used that year and a half to great advantage. Knowing that the attack might reach us in all too short a time, we immediately began greatly to increase our industrial strength and our capacity to meet the demands of modern warfare.

Precious months were gained by sending vast quantities of our war material to the nations of the world still able to resist Axis aggression. Our policy rested on the fundamental truth that the defense of any country resisting Hitler or Japan was in the long run, the defense of our own country. That policy has been justified. It has given us time, invaluable time, to build our American assembly lines of production.

Assembly lines are now in operation. Others are being rushed to completion. A steady stream of tanks and planes, of guns and ships, of shells and equipment— that is what these eighteen months have given us.

But it is all only a beginning of what has to be done. We must be set to face a long war against crafty and powerful bandits. The attack at Pearl Harbor can be repeated at any one of many points in both oceans and along both our coast lines and against all the rest of the hemisphere.

It will not only be a long war, it will be a hard war. That is the basis on which we now lay all our plans. That is the yardstick by which we measure what we shall need and demand: money, materials, doubled and quadrupled production—ever increasing. The production must be not only for our own Army and Navy and air forces. It must reinforce the other armies and navies and air forces fighting the Nazis and the war lords of Japan throughout the Americans and the world.

I have been working today on the subject of production. Your government has decided on two broad policies.

The first is to speed up all existing production by working on a seven-day-week basis in every war industry, including the production of essential raw materials .

The second policy, now being put into form, is to rush additions to the capacity of production by building more new plants, by adding to old plants, and by using the many smaller plants for war needs.

Over the hard road of the past months we have at times met obstacles and difficulties, division and disputes, indifference and callousness. That is now all past—and, I am sure, forgotten.

St. Bernard

You know that we are living in a time of chastisement and destruction. The laws of the land and the laws of Religion no longer have the strength to maintain the customs and stop the triumph of the evil ones. The devil of heresy is seated on the throne of truth. God has cursed His sanctuary.

All you who hear me, make haste to calm the wrath of Heaven! Leave off imploring His goodness with futile lamentations or mortifying yourself with disciplines, but rather take up your invincible shields. The clamor of arms, the dangers, difficulties, and fatigues of war— these are the penances that God imposes on you. Go to make reparation for your faults with victories against the infidels, and let the liberation of the Holy Places be the noble reward of your repentance.

If someone were to come and announce that the enemy had just entered your cities, stolen away your wives and children, and desecrated your churches, who would not immediately rush to take up arms? Well, all these evils and others still worse have fallen on the family of Jesus Christ, which is also yours. It was dispersed by the sword of pagans; barbarians destroyed the house of God and divided His inheritance. What else must take place for you to repair so many evils and avenge so many outrages?

Will you let the infidels contemplate in peace the destruction and looting they have done in the house of the Christian people? Think of how their triumph will be the cause of inconsolable sorrow for all centuries and an eternal shame for the generation that permitted it.

Yes, the living God has charged me with telling you that He will chastise all those who do not defend Him against His enemies. All of you, then, to arms! Let a holy ire animate you to combat, and let these words of the Prophet resound throughout the world: Cursed be he who does not bloody his sword!

If God calls you to defend Him, it is not because His hand has become any less powerful. Rather, God looks down at the children of man and wants to offer them the path of mercy; His goodness is giving you the day of forgiveness.

He chose you as the instrument of His revenge.

He wants to be indebted to you for the destruction of His enemies and the triumph of His justice.

Yes, the Omnipotent God calls you to make reparation for your sins by defending His glory and His name.

Christians warriors, these are combats worthy of you—combats that will attract the blessings of earth and Heaven, in which death itself will be for you but another triumph. Illustrious knights, remember the examples of your ancestors who conquered Jerusalem and whose names were inscribed in the Book of Life. Put on the Cross, which will earn you the conquest of the celestial kingdom.

Queen Elizabeth I of England

Message to Troops against the Spanish Armada
1588

My loving people, we have been persuaded by some, that are careful of our safety, to take heed how we commit ourselves to armed multitudes, for fear of treachery. But I assure you, I do not desire to live to distrust my faithful and loving people. Let tyrants fear; I have always so behaved myself that, under God, I have placed my chiefest strength and safeguard in the loyal hearts and good will of my subjects. And therefore, I am come amongst you at this time, not as for my recreation or sport, but being resolved, in the midst and heat of the battle, to live or die amongst you all; to lay down for my God and for my kingdom, and for my people, my honor and my blood, even the dust.

I know I have but the body of a weak and feeble woman; but I have the heart of a king, and of a king of England too; and think foul scorn that Parma or Spain, or any prince of Europe should dare to invade the borders of my realms: to which, rather than any dishonor should grow by me, I myself will take up arms; I myself will be your general, judge, and rewarder of every one of your virtues in the field.

I know already, by your forwardness, that you have deserved rewards and crowns; and we do assure you, on the word of a prince, they shall be duly paid you. In the mean, my lieutenant general shall be in my stead, than whom never prince commanded a more noble and worthy subject; not doubting by your obedience to my general, by your concord in the camp, and by your valor in the field—we shall shortly have a famous victory over the enemies of my God, of my kingdom, and of my people.

George W. Bush

Address on the Start of War in Iraq
March 20, 2003

My fellow citizens:

At this hour, American and coalition forces are in the early stages of military operations to disarm Iraq, to free its people and to defend the world from grave danger.

On my orders, coalition forces have begun striking selected targets of military importance to undermine Saddam Hussein's ability to wage war. These are opening stages of what will be a broad and concerted campaign.

More than 35 countries are giving crucial support from the use of naval and air bases to help with intelligence and logistics to deployment of combat units.

Every nation in this coalition has chosen to bear the duty and share the honor of serving in our common defense.

To all the men and women of the United States armed forces now in the Middle East, the peace of a troubled world and the hopes of an oppressed people now depend on you. That trust is well placed.

The enemies you confront will come to know your skill and bravery. The people you liberate will witness the honorable and decent spirit of the American military.

In this conflict, America faces an enemy that has no regard for conventions of war or rules of morality.

Saddam Hussein has placed Iraqi troops and equipment in civilian areas, attempting to use innocent men, women, and children as shields for his own military. A final atrocity against his people.

I want Americans and all the world to know that coalition forces will make every effort to spare innocent civilians from harm.

A campaign on the harsh terrain of the nation as large as California could be longer and more difficult than some predict, and helping Iraqis achieve a united, stable, and free country will require our sustained commitment.

We come to Iraq with respect for its citizens, for their great civilization, and for the religious faiths they practice. We have no ambition in Iraq except to remove a threat and restore control of that country to its own people.

I know that the families of our military are praying that all those who serve will return safely and soon.

Millions of Americans are praying with you for the safety of your loved ones and for the protection of the innocent.

For your sacrifice, you have the gratitude and respect of the American people and you can know that our forces will be coming home as soon as their work is done.

Our nation enters this conflict reluctantly, yet our purpose is sure. The people of the United States and our friends and allies will not live at the mercy of an outlaw regime that threatens the peace with weapons of mass murder.

We will meet that threat now with our army, air force, navy, coastguard and marines so that we do not have to meet it later with armies of firefighters and police and doctors on the streets of our cities.

Now that conflict has come, the only way to limit its duration is to apply decisive force and I assure you this will not be a campaign of half measures and we will accept no outcome but victory.

My fellow citizens, the dangers to our country and the world will be overcome. We will pass through this time of peril and carry on the work of peace. We will defend our freedom. We will bring freedom to others and we will prevail.

May God bless our country and all who defend her.

142

Richard M. Nixon

Vietnam Rally Speech: The Great Silent Majority
November 3, 1969

Good evening, my fellow Americans.

Tonight I want to talk to you on a subject of deep
concern to all Americans and to many people in all
parts of the world, the war in Vietnam.

I believe that one of the reasons for the deep division
about Vietnam is that many Americans have lost
confidence in what their Government has told them
about our policy. The American people cannot and
should not be asked to support a policy which involves
the overriding issues of war and peace unless they
know the truth about that policy.

Tonight, therefore, I would like to answer some of the
questions that I know are on the minds of many of you
listening to me.

How and why did America get involved in Vietnam in
the first place?

How has this administration changed the policy of the
previous Administration?

What has really happened in the negotiations in Paris
and on the battlefront in Vietnam?

What choices do we have if we are to end the war?

What are the prospects for peace?

Now let me begin by describing the situation I found when I was inaugurated on January 20: The war had been going on for four years. Thirty-one thousand Americans had been killed in action. The training program for the South Vietnamese was beyond schedule. Five hundred and forty-thousand Americans were in Vietnam, with no plans to reduce the number. No progress had been made at the negotiations in Paris, and the United States had not put forth a comprehensive peace proposal.

The war was causing deep division at home and criticism from many of our friends as well as our enemies abroad.

In view of these circumstances, there were some who urged that I end the war at once by ordering the immediate withdrawal of all American forces. From a political standpoint, this would have been a popular and easy course to follow. After all, we became involved in the war while my predecessor was in office. I could blame the defeat, which would be the result of my action, on him—and come out as the peacemaker. Some put it to me quite bluntly: This was the only way to avoid allowing Johnson's war to become Nixon's war.

But I had a greater obligation than to think only of the years of my Administration, and of the next election. I had to think of the effect of my decision on the next generation, and on the future of peace and freedom in America and in the world.

Let us all understand that the question before us is not whether some Americans are for peace and some Americans are against peace. The question at issue is not whether Johnson's war becomes Nixon's war. The great question is: How can we win America's peace?

Well, let us turn now to the fundamental issue: Why and how did the United States become involved in Vietnam in the first place? Fifteen years ago North Vietnam, with the logistical support of Communist China and the Soviet Union, launched a campaign to impose a Communist government on South Vietnam by instigating and supporting a revolution.

In response to the request of the Government of South Vietnam, President Eisenhower sent economic aid and military equipment to assist the people of South Vietnam in their efforts to prevent a Communist takeover. Seven years ago, President Kennedy sent 16,000 military personnel to Vietnam as combat advisers. Four years ago, President Johnson sent American combat forces to South Vietnam.

Now many believe that President Johnson's decision to send American combat forces to South Vietnam was wrong. And many others, I among them, have been strongly critical of the way the war has been conducted.

But the question facing us today is: Now that we are in the war, what is the best way to end it?

In January, I could only conclude that the precipitate withdrawal of all American forces from Vietnam would be a disaster not only for South Vietnam but for the United States and for the cause of peace.

For the South Vietnamese, our precipitate withdrawal would inevitably allow the Communists to repeat the massacres which followed their takeover in the North, 15 years before. They then murdered more than 50,000 people, and hundreds of thousands more died in slave labor camps.

We saw a prelude of what would happen in South Vietnam when the Communists entered the city of Hue last year. During their brief rule there, there was a bloody reign of terror in which 3,000 civilians were clubbed, shot to death, and buried in mass graves.

With the sudden collapse of our support, these atrocities at Hue would become the nightmare of the entire nation and particularly for the million-and-a half Catholic refugees who fled to South Vietnam when the Communists took over in the North.

For the United States this first defeat in our nation's history would result in a collapse of confidence in

146

American leadership not only in Asia but throughout the world.

Three American Presidents have recognized the great stakes involved in Vietnam and understood what had to be done.

In 1963, President Kennedy with his characteristic eloquence and clarity said,

> "We want to see a stable Government there. We believe strongly in that. We are not going to withdraw from that effort. In my opinion, for us to withdraw from that effort would mean a collapse not only of South Vietnam but Southeast Asia. So we're going to stay there."

President Eisenhower and President Johnson expressed the same conclusion during their terms of office.

For the future of peace, precipitate withdrawal would be a disaster of immense magnitude. A nation cannot remain great if it betrays its allies and lets down its friends. Our defeat and humiliation in South Vietnam without question would promote recklessness in the councils of those great powers who have not yet abandoned their goals of worlds conquest. This would spark violence wherever our commitments help maintain the peace—in the Middle East, in Berlin, eventually even in the Western Hemisphere. Ultimately, this would cost more lives. It would not bring peace. It would bring more war.

For these reasons, I rejected the recommendation that I should end the war by immediately withdrawing all of our forces. I chose instead to change American policy on both the negotiating front and the battle front in order to end the war fought on many fronts. I initiated a pursuit for peace on many fronts. In a television speech on May 14, in a speech before the United Nations, on a number of other occasions, I set forth our peace proposals in great detail.

We have offered the complete withdrawal of all outside forces within one year. We have proposed a cease-fire under international supervision. We have offered free elections under international supervision with the Communists participating in the organization and conduct of the elections as an organized political force. And the Saigon government has pledged to accept the result of the election.

We have not put forth our proposals on a take-it-or-leave-it basis. We have indicated that we're willing to discuss the proposals that have been put forth by the other side. We have declared that anything is negotiable, except the right of the people of South Vietnam to determine their own future.

At the Paris peace conference, Ambassador Lodge has demonstrated our flexibility and good faith in 40 public meetings. Hanoi has refused even to discuss our proposals. They demand our unconditional acceptance of their terms, which are that we withdraw all American forces immediately and unconditionally, and that we overthrow the government of South Vietnam as we leave.

We have not limited our peace initiatives to public forums and public statements. I recognized in January that a long and bitter war like this usually cannot be settled in a public forum. That is why in addition to the public statements and negotiations, I have explored every possible private avenue that might lead to a settlement.

Tonight, I am taking the unprecedented step of disclosing to you some of our other initiatives for peace, initiatives we undertook privately and secretly because we thought we thereby might open a door, which publicly would be closed.

I did not wait for my inauguration to begin my quest for peace. Soon after my election, through an individual who was directly in contact on a personal basis with the leaders of North Vietnam, I made two private offers for a rapid, comprehensive settlement. Hanoi's replies called in effect for our surrender before negotiations. Since the Soviet Union furnishes most of the military equipment for North Vietnam, Secretary of State Rogers, my assistant for national security affairs, Dr. Kissinger, Ambassador Lodge, and I personally have met on a number of occasions with representatives of the Soviet Government to enlist their assistance in getting meaningful negotiations started. In addition, we have had extended discussions directed toward that same end with representatives of

149

other governments which have diplomatic relations with North Vietnam.

None of these initiatives have to date produced results. In mid-July, I became convinced that it was necessary to make a major move to break the deadlock in the Paris talks. I spoke directly in this office, where I'm now sitting, with an individual who had known Ho Chi Minh on a personal basis for 25 years. Through him, I sent a letter to Ho Chi Minh. I did this outside of the usual diplomatic channels with the hope that with the necessity of making statements for propaganda removed, there might be constructive progress toward bringing the war to an end.

Let me read from that letter to you now:

"Dear Mr. President:

I realize that it is difficult to communicate meaningfully across the gulf of four years of war. But precisely because of this gulf I wanted to take this opportunity to reaffirm in all solemnity my desire to work for a just peace. I deeply believe that the war in Vietnam has gone on too long and delay in bringing it to an end can benefit no one, least of all the people of Vietnam. The time has come to move forward at the conference table toward an early resolution of this tragic war. You will find us forthcoming and open-minded in a common effort to bring the blessings of peace to the brave people of Vietnam. Let history record that at this critical juncture, both sides turned their face toward peace rather than toward conflict and war."

I received Ho Chi Minh's reply on August 30, three days before his death. It simply reiterated the public position North Vietnam had taken at Paris and flatly rejected my initiative. The full text of both letters is being released to the press.

In addition to the public meetings that I have referred to, Ambassador Lodge has met with Vietnam's chief negotiator in Paris in 11 private sessions. And we have taken other significant initiatives which must remain secret to keep open some channels of communications which may still prove to be productive.

But the effect of all the public, private, and secret negotiations which have been undertaken since the bombing halt a year ago, and since this Administration came into office on January 20th, can be summed up in one sentence: No progress whatever has been made except agreement on the shape of the bargaining table.

Well, now, who's at fault? It's become clear that the obstacle in negotiating an end to the war is not the President of the United States. It is not the South Vietnamese Government. The obstacle is the other side's absolute refusal to show the least willingness to join us in seeking a just peace. And it will not do so while it is convinced that all it has to do is to wait for our next concession, and our next concession after that one, until it gets everything it wants.

There can now be no longer any question that progress in negotiation depends only on Hanoi 's deciding to negotiate—to negotiate seriously. I realize that this report on our efforts on the diplomatic front is discouraging to the American people, but the American people are entitled to know the truth—the bad news as well as the good news—where the lives of our young men are involved.

Now let me turn, however, to a more encouraging report on another front. At the time we launched our search for peace, I recognized we might not succeed in bringing an end to the war through negotiations. I therefore put into effect another plan to bring peace— a plan which will bring the war to an end regardless of what happens on the negotiating front. It is in line with the major shift in U. S. foreign policy which I described in my press conference at Guam on July 25. Let me briefly explain what has been described as the Nixon Doctrine—a policy which not only will help end the war in Vietnam, but which is an essential element of our program to prevent future Vietnams.

We Americans are a do-it-yourself people—we're an impatient people. Instead of teaching someone else to do a job, we like to do it ourselves. And this trait has been carried over into our foreign policy. In Korea and again in Vietnam, the United States furnished most of the money, most of the arms, and most of the men to help the people of those countries defend their freedom against Communist aggression.

Before any American troops were committed to Vietnam, a leader of another Asian country expressed this opinion to me when I was traveling in Asia as a private citizen. He said: "When you are trying to assist another nation defend its freedom, U.S. policy should be to help them fight the war, but not to fight the war for them."

Well in accordance with this wise counsel, I laid down in Guam three principles as guidelines for future American policy toward Asia. First, the United States will keep all of its treaty commitments. Second, we shall provide a shield if a nuclear power threatens the freedom of a nation allied with us, or of a nation whose survival we consider vital to our security. Third, in cases involving other types of aggression we shall furnish military and economic assistance when requested in accordance with our treaty commitments. But we shall look to the nation directly threatened to assume the primary responsibility of providing the manpower for its defense.

After I announced this policy, I found that the leaders of the Philippines, Thailand, Vietnam, South Korea, other nations which might be threatened by Communist aggression, welcomed this new direction in American foreign policy.

The defense of freedom is everybody's business—not just America's business. And it is particularly the responsibility of the people whose freedom is threatened. In the previous Administration, we Americanized the war in Vietnam. In this Administration, we are Vietnamizing the search for peace.

The policy of the previous Administration not only resulted in our assuming the primary responsibility for fighting the war, but even more significant did not adequately stress the goal of strengthening the South Vietnamese so that they could defend themselves when we left.

The Vietnamization plan was launched following Secretary Laird's visit to Vietnam in March. Under the plan, I ordered first a substantial increase in the training and equipment of South Vietnamese forces. In July, on my visit to Vietnam, I changed General Abrams's orders, so that they were consistent with the objectives of our new policies. Under the new orders, the primary mission of our troops is to enable the South Vietnamese forces to assume the full responsibility for the security of South Vietnam. Our air operations have been reduced by over 20 per cent.

And now we have begun to see the results of this long-overdue change in American policy in Vietnam. After five years of Americans going into Vietnam we are finally bringing American men home. By December 15, over 60,000 men will have been withdrawn from South

Vietnam, including 20 percent of all of our combat forces. The South Vietnamese have continued to gain in strength. As a result, they've been able to take over combat responsibilities from our American troops.

Two other significant developments have occurred since this Administration took office. Enemy infiltration—infiltration which is essential if they are to launch a major attack over the last three months—is less than 20 percent of what it was over the same period last year. And most important, United States casualties have declined during the last two months to the lowest point in three years.

Let me now turn to our program for the future. We have adopted a plan which we have worked out in cooperation with the South Vietnamese for the complete withdrawal of all U.S. combat ground forces and their replacement by South Vietnamese forces on an orderly scheduled timetable. This withdrawal will be made from strength and not from weakness. As South Vietnamese forces become stronger, the rate of American withdrawal can become greater.

I have not, and do not, intend to announce the timetable for our program, and there are obvious reasons for this decision, which I'm sure you will understand. As I've indicated on several occasions, the rate of withdrawal will depend on developments on three fronts. One of these is the progress which can be, or might be, made in the Paris talks. An announcement of a fixed timetable for our withdrawal would completely remove any incentive for the enemy to negotiate an agreement. They would simply wait until our forces had withdrawn and then move in.

The other two factors on which we will base our withdrawal decisions are the level of enemy activity and the progress of the training programs of the South Vietnamese forces. And I am glad to be able to report tonight, progress on both of these fronts has been greater than we anticipated when we started the program in June for withdrawal. As a result, our timetable for withdrawal is more optimistic now than when we made our first estimates in June.

Now this clearly demonstrates why it is not wise to be frozen in on a fixed timetable. We must retain the flexibility to base each withdrawal decision on the situation as it is at that time, rather than on estimates that are no longer valid. Along with this optimistic estimate, I must in all candor, leave one note of caution. If the level of enemy activity significantly increases, we might have to adjust our timetable accordingly.

However, I want the record to be completely clear on one point. At the time of the bombing halt just a year ago there was some confusion as to whether there was an understanding on the part of the enemy—that if we stopped the bombing of North Vietnam, they would stop the shelling of cities in South Vietnam.

156

I want to be sure that there is no misunderstanding on the part of the enemy with regard to our withdrawal program. We have noted the reduced level of infiltration, the reduction of our casualties and are basing our withdrawal decisions partially on those factors. If the level of infiltration or our casualties increase while we are trying to scale down the fighting, it will be the result of a conscious decision by the enemy. Hanoi could make no greater mistake than to assume that an increase in violence will be to its advantage.

If I conclude that increased enemy action jeopardizes our remaining forces in Vietnam, I shall not hesitate to take strong and effective measures to deal with that situation. This is not a threat. This is a statement of policy, which as Commander-in-Chief of our armed forces, I am making and meeting my responsibility for the protection of American fighting men wherever they may be.

My fellow Americans, I am sure you can recognize from what I have said that we really only have two choices open to us if we want to end this war. I can order an immediate precipitate withdrawal of all Americans from Vietnam without regard to the effects of that action. Or we can persist in our search for a just peace through a negotiated settlement, if possible, or through continued implementation of our plan for Vietnamization, if necessary—a plan in which we will withdraw all of our forces from Vietnam on a schedule in accordance with our program as the South

Vietnamese become strong enough to defend their own freedom.

I have chosen this second course. It is not the easy way. It is the right way. It is a plan which will end the war and serve the cause of peace, not just in Vietnam but in the Pacific and in the world.

In speaking of the consequences of a precipitous withdrawal, I mentioned that our allies would lose confidence in America. Far more dangerous, we would lose confidence in ourselves. Oh, the immediate reaction would be a sense of relief that our men were coming home. But as we saw the consequences of what we had done, inevitable remorse and divisive recrimination would scar our spirit as a people.

We have faced other crises in our history, and we have become stronger by rejecting the easy way out and taking the right way in meeting our challenges. Our greatness as a nation has been our capacity to do what has to be done when we knew our course was right. I recognize that some of my fellow citizens disagree with the plan for peace I have chosen. Honest and patriotic Americans have reached different conclusions as to how peace should be achieved. In San Francisco a few weeks ago, I saw demonstrators carrying signs reading, "Lose in Vietnam, bring the boys home." Well, one of the strengths of our free society is that any American has a right to reach that conclusion and to advocate that point of view.

But as President of the United States, I would be untrue to my oath of office if I allowed the policy of this nation to be dictated by the minority who hold that point of view and who try to impose it on the nation by mounting demonstrations in the street. For almost 200 years, the policy of this nation has been made under our Constitution by those leaders in the Congress and the White House elected by all the people. If a vocal minority, however fervent its cause, prevails over reason and the will of the majority, this nation has no future as a free society.

And now, I would like to address a word, if I may. To the young people of this nation who are particularly concerned, and I understand why they are concerned, about this war: I respect your idealism. I share your concern for peace. I want peace as much as you do. There are powerful personal reasons I want to end this war. This week I will have to sign 83 letters to mothers, fathers, wives, and loved ones of men who have given their lives for America in Vietnam. It's very little satisfaction to me that this is only one-third as many letters as I signed the first week in office. There is nothing I want more than to see the day come when I do not have to write any of those letters.

I want to end the war to save the lives of those brave young men in Vietnam, but I want to end it in a way which will increase the chance that their younger brothers and their sons will not have to fight in some future Vietnam some place in the world.

And I want to end the war for another reason. I want to end it so that the energy and dedication of you, our young people, now too often directed into bitter hatred against those responsible for the war, can be turned to the great challenges of peace, a better life for all Americans, a better life for all people on this earth.

I have chosen a plan for peace. I believe it will succeed. If it does not succeed, what the critics say now won't matter. Or if it does succeed, what the critics say now won't matter. If it does not succeed, anything I say then won't matter.

I know it may not be fashionable to speak of patriotism or national destiny these days, but I feel it is appropriate to do so on this occasion. Two hundred years ago, this nation was weak and poor. But even then, America was the hope of millions in the world. Today we have become the strongest and richest nation in the world, and the wheel of destiny has turned so that any hope the world has for the survival of peace and freedom will be determined by whether the American people have the moral stamina and the courage to meet the challenge of free-world leadership.

Let historians not record that when America was the most powerful nation in the world, we passed on the other side of the road and allowed the last hopes for peace and freedom of millions of people to be suffocated by the forces of totalitarianism.

160

So tonight, to you, the great silent majority of my fellow Americans, I ask for your support. I pledged in my campaign for the Presidency to end the war in a way that we could win the peace. I have initiated a plan of action which will enable me to keep that pledge. The more support I can have from the American people, the sooner that pledge can be redeemed. For the more divided we are at home, the less likely the enemy is to negotiate at Paris.

Let us be united for peace. Let us also be united against defeat. Because let us understand—North Vietnam cannot defeat or humiliate the United States. Only Americans can do that.

Fifty years ago, in this room and at this very desk, President Woodrow Wilson spoke words which caught the imagination of a war-weary world. He said: "This is the war to end wars." His dream for peace after World War I was shattered on the hard reality of great power politics. And Woodrow Wilson died a broken man.

Tonight, I do not tell you that the war in Vietnam is the war to end wars, but I do say this: I have initiated a plan which will end this war in a way that will bring us closer to that great goal to which Woodrow Wilson and every American President in our history has been dedicated—the goal of a just and lasting peace.

As President, I hold the responsibility for choosing the best path for that goal and then leading the nation along it.

I pledge to you tonight that I shall meet this responsibility with all of the strength and wisdom I can command in accordance with your hopes, mindful of your concerns, sustained by your prayers.

Thank you and good night.

Vladimir Lenin

World War One
February 8, 1916

Comrades! The European war has been raging for more than eighteen months. And as each month, as each day of the war goes by, it becomes clearer and clearer to the masses of the workers that the Zimmerwald Manifesto expressed the truth when it declared that phrases about "defense of the fatherland" and the like are nothing but capitalist deception.

It is becoming more evident every day that this is a war between capitalists, between big robbers, who are quarrelling over the loot, each striving to obtain the largest share, the largest number of countries to plunder, and the largest number of nations to suppress and enslave.

It may sound incredible, especially to Swiss comrades, but it is nevertheless true that in Russia, also, not only bloody tsarism, not only the capitalists, but also a section of the so-called or ex-Socialists say that Russia is fighting a "war of defense," that Russia is only fighting against German invasion.

The whole world knows, however, that for decades, tsarism has been oppressing more than a hundred million people belonging to other nationalities in

Russia; that for decades, Russia has been pursuing a predatory policy towards China, Persia, Armenia, and Galicia. Neither Russia, nor Germany, nor any other Great Power has the right to claim that it is waging a "war of defense."

All the Great Powers are waging an imperialist, capitalist war, a predatory war, a war for the oppression of small and foreign nations, a war for the sake of the profits of the capitalists, who are coining golden profits amounting to billions out of the appalling sufferings of the masses, out of the blood of the proletariat.

Four years ago, in November 1912, when it had become clear that war was approaching, the representatives of the Socialist Parties of the whole world gathered at the International Socialist Congress in Basle. Even at that time, there was no room for doubt that the impending war would be a war between the Great Powers, between the great beasts of prey; that responsibility for the war would rest upon the governments and the capitalist classes of all the Great Powers.

The Basle Manifesto, which was adopted unanimously by the Socialist Parties of the whole world, openly stated this truth. The Basle Manifesto does not say a word about a "war of defense," or "defense of the fatherland." It castigates the governments and the bourgeoisie of all the Great Powers without exception. It said openly that war would be the greatest of crimes, that the workers would consider it a crime to shoot at each other, that the horrors of war and the indignation these would rouse among the workers would inevitably lead to a proletarian revolution.

When the war actually broke out, it was realized that its character had been correctly defined at Basle. But the Socialist and labor organizations were not unanimous in carrying out the Basle decisions; they split. We see now, that in all countries of the world, the Socialist and labor organizations are split into two big camps. The smaller section, the leaders, functionaries and officials, have betrayed Socialism and have deserted to the side of the governments. Another section, to which the mass of class conscious workers belong, continues to gather its forces, to fight against the war and for the proletarian revolution.

The views of this latter section also found expression in the Zimmerwald Manifesto.

In Russia, from the very beginning of the war, the workers' deputies in the Duma, waged a determined revolutionary struggle against the war and the tsarist monarchy. Five workers' deputies—Petrovsky, Badayev, Muranov, Shagov and Samoilov—distributed revolutionary manifestoes against the war and energetically carried on revolutionary agitation. Tsarism ordered the arrest of those five deputies, put them on trial, and sentenced them to lifelong exile in Siberia. For months, the leaders of the working class of Russia have been pining in Siberia; but their cause has not gone   under; their work is being continued by the class-conscious workers all over Russia.

Comrades! You have heard the speeches of representatives of various countries, who have told you about the workers' revolutionary struggle against the war. I merely want to quote one other example from that great and rich country, the United States of America.

The capitalists of that country are now making enormous profits out of the European war. And they, too, are agitating for war. They say that America must also prepare to take part in the war. Hundreds of millions of dollars must be squeezed out of the people for new armaments, for armaments without end. And in America, too, a section of the Socialists echoes this false, criminal call. Let me read to you what Comrade Eugene Debs, the most popular leader of the American Socialists, the Presidential candidate of the American Socialist Party, writes.

In the September 11, 1915, American weekly, *The Appeal to Reason,* he says: "*I am not a capitalist soldier; I am a proletarian revolutionist. I do not belong to the regular army of rite plutocracy, but to the irregular army of the people. I refuse to obey any command to fight for the ruling class.... I am opposed to every war but one; I am for that war with heart and soul, and that is the world-wide war of the social revolution. In that war I am prepared to fight in any way the ruling class may make it necessary....*"

166

This is what Eugene Debs, the American Rebel, the beloved leader of the American workers, writes to them.

This again shows you, comrades, that in all countries of the world real preparations are being made to rally the forces of the working class. The horrors of war and the sufferings of the people are incredible. But we must not, and we have no reason whatever, to view the future with despair.

The millions of victims who will fall in the war, and as a consequence of the war, will not fall in vain. The millions who are starving, the millions who are sacrificing their lives in the trenches, are not only suffering, they are also gathering strength, are pondering over the real cause of the war, are becoming more determined, and are acquiring a clearer revolutionary understanding.

Rising discontent of the masses, growing ferment, strikes, demonstrations,   protests against the war—all this is taking place in *all* countries of the world. And this is the guarantee that the European War will be followed by the proletarian revolution against capitalism.

George Patton, Jr.

On the Eve of Invasion of France in World War II
June 5, 1944

We become operational officially tomorrow, and doubtless from time to time there will be some complaints that we are punishing people too hard. I don't give a good goddam about such complaints. I believe in the old and sound rule that an ounce of sweat is worth a gallon of blood.

The harder we push, the more Germans we'll kill, and the more Germans we kill, the fewer of our men will be killed. Pushing means lower casualties. I want you to remember that.

There is another thing I want you to remember. Forget this goddamed business of worrying about our flanks. We must guard our flanks, but not to the extent that we don't do anything else. Some goddam fool once said that flanks must be secured, and since then sons-of-bitches all over the world have been going crazy guarding their flanks. Flanks are something for the enemy to worry about, not us.

Also, I don't want any messages saying, "I am holding my position." We're not holding anything. Let the Hun do that. We are advancing constantly and are not interested in holding anything, except onto the enemy.

168

We're trying to hold onto him and kick the hell out of him all the time.

Our basic plan of operation is to advance and to keep on advancing regardless of whether we have to go over, under, or through the enemy. We have one motto, "Audacious, audacious, always audacious." Remember that. From here on out, until we win or die in the attempt, we will always be audacious.

George Washington

Insurrection
March 15, 1783

Gentlemen:

By an anonymous summons, an attempt has been made to convene you together; how inconsistent with the rules of propriety, how unmilitary, and how subversive of all order and discipline, let the good sense of the army decide.

Thus much, gentlemen, I have thought it incumbent on me to observe to you, to show upon what principles I opposed the irregular and hasty meeting which was proposed to have been held on Tuesday last—and not because I wanted a disposition to give you every opportunity consistent with your own honor, and the dignity of the army, to make known your grievances.

If my conduct heretofore has not evinced to you that I have been a faithful friend to the army, my declaration of it at this time would be equally unavailing and improper. But as I was among the first who embarked in the cause of our common country.

As I have never left your side one moment, but when called from you on public duty.

As I have been the constant companion and witness of your distresses, and not among the last to feel and acknowledge your merits.

As I have ever considered my own military reputation as inseparably connected with that of the army.

As my heart has ever expanded with joy when I have heard its praises, and my indignation has arisen when the mouth of detraction has been opened against it—it can scarcely be supposed, at this late stage of the war, that I am indifferent to its interests.

But how are they to be promoted? The way is plain, says the anonymous addresser. If war continues, remove into the unsettled country, there establish yourselves, and leave an ungrateful country to defend itself.

But who are they to defend? Our wives, our children, our farms, and other property which we leave behind us. Or, in this state of hostile separation, are we to take the two first (the latter cannot be removed) to perish in a wilderness, with hunger, cold, and nakedness?

If peace takes place, never sheathe your swords, says he, until you have obtained full and ample justice; this dreadful alternative, of either deserting our country in the extremest hour of her distress or turning our arms against it—which is the apparent object, unless Congress can be compelled into instant compliance—

has something so shocking in it that humanity revolts at the idea.

My God! What can this writer have in view, by recommending such measures? Can he be a friend to the army? Can he be a friend to this country? Rather, is he not an insidious foe? Some emissary, perhaps, from New York, plotting the ruin of both, by sowing the seeds of discord and separation between the civil and military powers of the continent? And what a compliment does he pay to our understandings when he recommends measures in either alternative, impracticable in their nature?

I cannot, in justice to my own belief, and what I have great reason to conceive is the intention of Congress, conclude this address, without giving it as my decided opinion, that that honorable body entertain exalted sentiments of the services of the army; and from a full conviction of its merits and sufferings, will do it complete justice. That their endeavors to discover and establish funds for this purpose have been unwearied, and will not cease till they have succeeded, I have not a doubt.

But, like all other large bodies, where there is a variety of different interests to reconcile, their deliberations are slow. Why, then, should we distrust them? And, in consequence of that distrust, adopt measures which may cast a shade over that glory which has been so justly acquired; and tarnish the reputation of an army which is celebrated through all Europe, for its fortitude and patriotism? And for what is this done? To bring the object we seek nearer? No! Most certainly, in my opinion, it will cast it at a greater distance.

For myself—and I take no merit in giving the assurance, being induced to it from principles of gratitude, veracity, and justice—a grateful sense of the confidence you have ever placed in me, a recollection of the cheerful assistance and prompt obedience I have experienced from you, under every vicissitude of fortune, and the sincere affection I feel for an army I have so long had the honor to command, will oblige me to declare, in this public and solemn manner, that in the attainment of complete justice for all your toils and dangers, and in the gratification of every wish, so far as may be done consistently with the great duty I owe my country and those powers we are bound to respect, you may freely command my services to the utmost of my abilities.

While I give you these assurances, and pledge myself in the most unequivocal manner to exert whatever ability I am possessed of in your favor, let me entreat you, gentlemen, on your part, not to take any measures which, viewed in the calm light of reason, will lessen the dignity and sully the glory you have hitherto maintained; let me request you to rely on the plighted faith of your country, and place a full confidence in the purity of the intentions of Congress; that previous to your dissolution as an army, they will cause all your accounts to be fairly liquidated, as directed in their resolutions, which were published to you two days ago,

173

and that they will adopt the most effectual measures in their power to render ample justice to you, for your faithful and meritorious services.

And let me conjure you, in the name of our common country—as you value your own sacred honor, as you respect the rights of humanity, and as you regard the military and national character of America—to express your utmost horror and detestation of the man who wishes, under any specious pretenses, to overturn the liberties of our country, and who wickedly attempts to open the floodgates of civil discord, and deluge our rising empire in blood.

By thus determining and thus acting, you will pursue the plain and direct road to the attainment of your wishes. You will defeat the insidious designs of our enemies, who are compelled to resort from open force to secret artifice. You will give one more distinguished proof of unexampled patriotism and patient virtue, rising superior to the pressure of the most complicated sufferings. And you will, by the dignity of your conduct, afford occasion for posterity to say, when speaking of the glorious example you have exhibited to mankind, "Had this day been wanting, the world had never seen the last stage of perfection to which human nature is capable of attaining."

Index